ART BOOKS

FROM CRESCENT MOON PUBLISHING

Leonardo da Vinci
by James Pearson

Early Netherlandish Painting
by Rosalind Mutter

Piero della Francesca
by Naomi Haskell

Giovanni Bellini
by Julia Davis

Eric Gill: Nuptials of God
by Anthony Hoyland

Minimal Art and Artists In the 1960s and After
by Laura Garrard

Postwar Art
by George Knighton

Vincent van Gogh: Visionary Landscapes
by Stuart Morris

Max Beckmann
by Stuart Morris

Egon Schiele: Sex and Death in Purple Stockings
by D. Simon Eade

Mark Rothko: The Art of Transcendence
by Julia Davis

Jasper Johns
by L.M. Poole

Brice Marden
by Laura Garrard

Frank Stella: American Abstract Artist
by James Pearson

The Light Eternal: J.M.W. Turner
by Jeremy Mark Robinson

Maurice Sendak and the Art of Children's Book Illustration
by L.M. Poole

Sex in Art: Pornography and Pleasure in Painting and Sculpture
by Cassidy Hughes

Glorification: Religious Abstraction
In Renaissance and 20th Century Painting
by Jeremy Mark Robinson

The Art of Andy Goldsworthy
by William Malpas

Andy Goldsworthy: Touching Nature
by William Malpas

Andy Goldsworthy In Close-Up
by William Malpas

The Art of Richard Long
by William Malpas

Constantin Brancusi: Sculpting the Essence of Things
by James Pearson

Alison Wilding: The Embrace of Sculpture
by Susan Quinnell

The Erotic Object: Sexuality in Sculpture
From Prehistory to the Present Day
by Susan Quinnell

Land Art: A Complete Guide to Landscape, Environmental,
Earthworks, Nature, Sculpture and Installation Art
by William Malpas

Land Art In Close-Up
by William Malpas

Colourfield Painting: Minimal, Cool, Hard Edge, Serial
and Post-Painterly Abstract Art From the Sixties to the Present
by Laura Garrard

INGRES

INGRES

A. J. FINBERG

CRESCENT MOON

First published 1910. This edition © 2017.

Printed and bound in the U.S.A.
Set in Book Antiqua 10 on 14pt.
Designed by Radiance Graphics.

Thanks to the authors and publishers quoted.

British Library Cataloguing in Publication data

ISBN-13 9781861716378

CRESCENT MOON PUBLISHING
P.O. Box 1312, Maidstone, Kent, ME14 5XU
Great Britain, www.crmoon.com

Contents

NOTE ON THE TEXT

The text is from *Ingres* by A.J. Finberg, published by Frederick Stokes, New York, 1910.

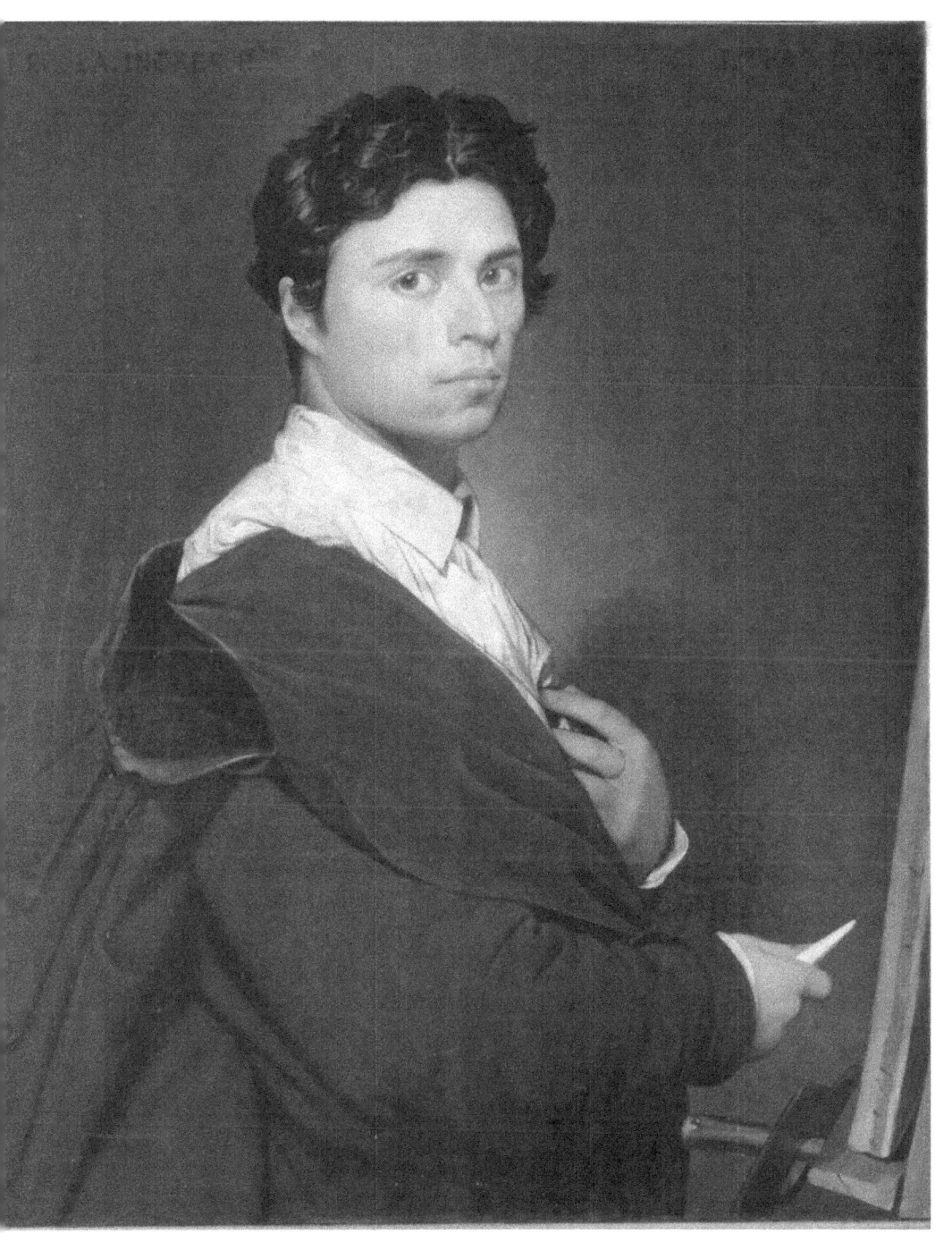

J.A.D. Ingres, Self-Portrait, 1804, Louvre

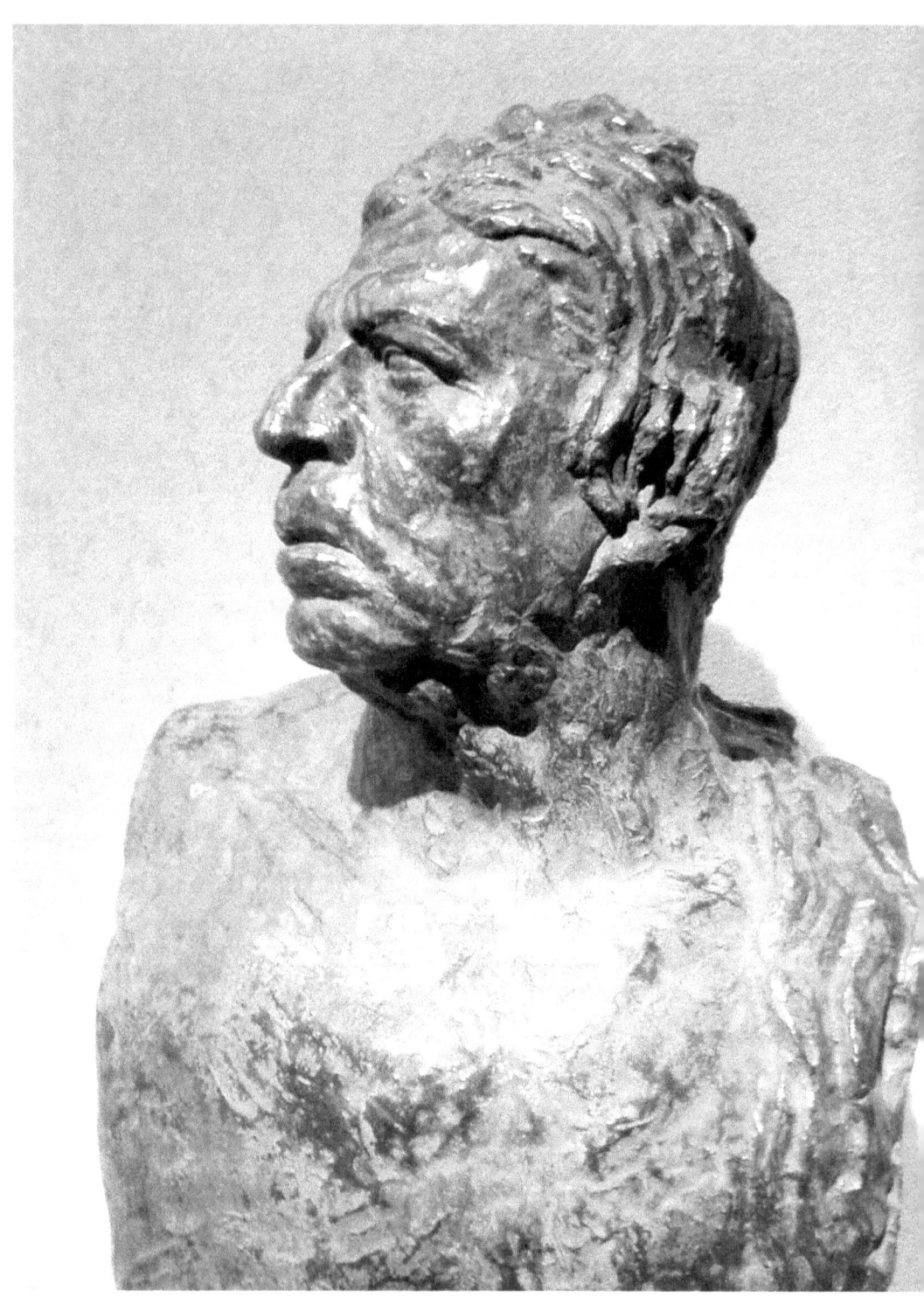

Antoine Bourdelle, Ingres, Musée Antoine Bourdelle

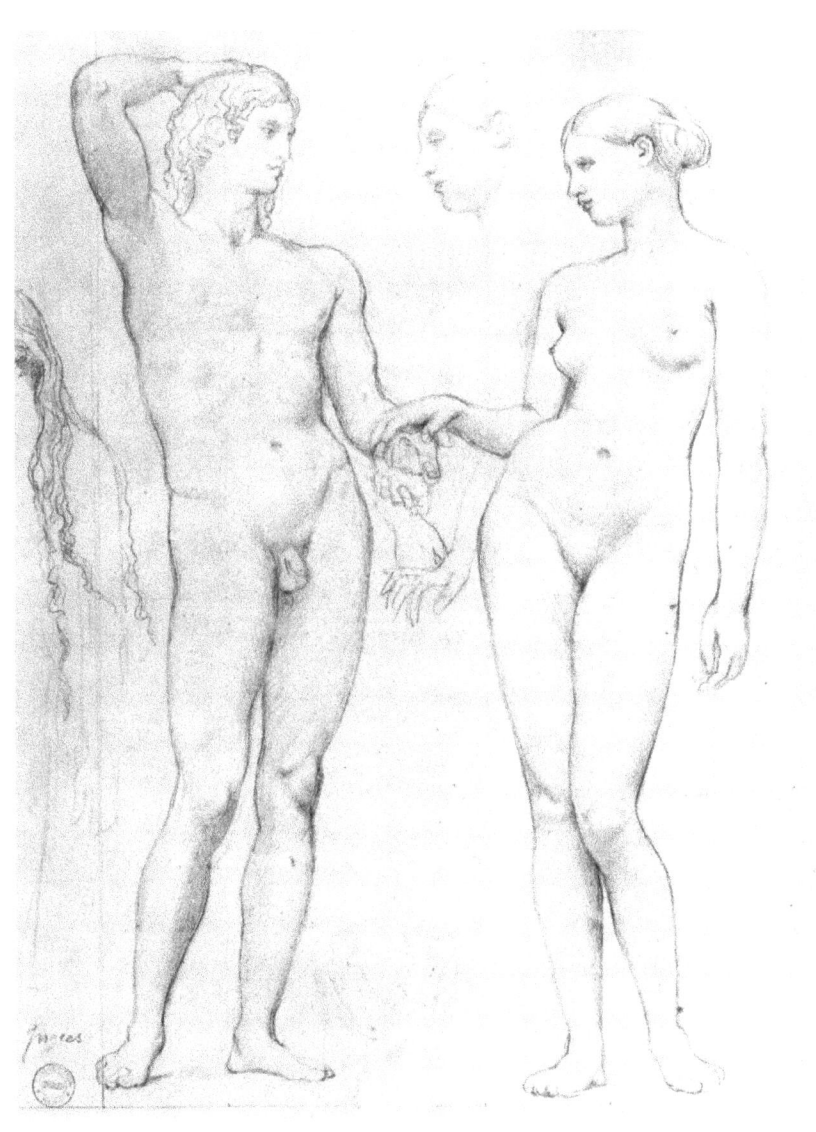

J.A.D. Ingres, Study For L'Age d'Or, 1862

Jean-Auguste-Dominique Ingres was born on the 29th August 1778, at Montauban. A stranger birthplace for a great artist could hardly be found. All the passion not absorbed in the material cares of life there turns to fanaticism. Religious hatred runs high. The municipal elections are fought out on religious grounds. Protestant and Roman Catholic hate but do not know one another. Each family lives for itself and by itself. A visit is said to be considered as an indiscretion. And nature there does nothing to soften the heart or the manners of man. The soil is dusty on the surface and hard to dig. The local colour is sombre, the general aspect of things sad. In the cold, dull light the forms detach themselves without grace or sympathy. The people have squat, thick-set figures, with round heads and heavy jaws. Their souls are as sombre and hard as their faces. They have ardour, but it is all concentrated and suppressed, burning within them like a brazier without flames. They show an extreme eagerness for work and gain; a silent obstinacy is the leading trait of their character. Ingres' mother belonged to these parts and to this race, and from her he seems to have derived a part of his stormy and inflexible, his unquiet and haughty genius.

Ingres' father came from Toulouse. Little more than three miles separate Toulouse from Montauban, but the chain of little hills which throws off, to the left, the river Garonne, and to the right the Tarn and the Aveyron, serves as the dividing line of two profoundly different regions and races. In contrast with the sterile and rocky regions of the North, the plains of Languedoc, with their great river and verdant meadows, seem a land of joy and enchantment. It was at Toulouse, with its courts of love, its floral fêtes, its contests of song and poetry, that Ingres' father was born. If we may judge from the portrait which Ingres painted of him (it is preserved at the Museum of Montauban), his father must have been an uncommon man. As we see him in this portrait he has a fine forehead, with big black eyes, and a look full of frankness and penetration. The evidence of this portrait is confirmed by the following letter, written by Ingres towards the end of his life, to a gentleman who had asked him for information about his father:–

"Sir, – Jean-Marie-Joseph Ingres was born at Toulouse (in 1734): his father, whom I saw in my childhood, was a master tailor; he lived to a great age. My father when he was very young entered the Academy of Toulouse. He had as master, I believe, M. Lucas, a celebrated sculptor, a professor of the said Academy. Later he went to Marseille, then settled at Montauban and married my mother, Anne Moulet, on 12th August 1777. He was very much loved and appreciated by the leading families of the city and by Mgr. de Breteuil, the Bishop of Montauban, of whom he made a large medallion in profile. This bishop employed my father a great deal at his palace and in his country house, situated near the city.

"My father was born with a rare genius for the fine arts. I say the fine arts because he executed painting, sculpture, and even architecture with success. I saw him construct an important building in our principal street.

"If M. Ingres had had the same advantages which he gave his son, of going to Paris to study under the greatest of our masters, he would have been the first artist of his time. My father, who drew perfectly, painted also in miniature. He also painted views of the country from nature….

"Nothing came amiss to him. In sculpture his work ranged from the sphinxes and figures of abbés reading, which were placed in gardens, to the colossal statues of Liberty which he was forced to improvise in our temples for the Republican fêtes. He made with the greatest facility ornaments of all kinds, with which he decorated most tastefully the buildings of his time…. Finally, he attracted everybody by his lovable character, his goodness, his eminently artistic tastes. Every one was anxious to enjoy his society.

"He often went to Toulouse, his native place, to renew his strength, so to speak, in that large and beautiful city, almost as rich then in monuments of art as Rome, which it greatly resembles. He loved to find himself again with the friends of his youth, all distinguished artists. He took me often with him in these short journeys.

"Without being a musician, my father adored music, and sang very well with a tenor voice. He gave me his taste for music and made me learn to play the violin. I succeeded well enough with it to be admitted into the orchestra of the Grand Theatre of Toulouse, where I played a concerto of Viotti with success...."

In this glowing eulogy of his father there is doubtless a certain amount of pious exaggeration. The man was a true Toulousian, a fine singer, an occasional performer on the violin, an improviser in everything, with a natural gift for drawing and a plastic sense common among his compatriots. That he would have been "one of the first artists of his time" if he had had the advantage of studying in Paris is manifestly absurd. His work shows a want of vigour, of originality, of invention. He had a certain correctness of eye and skill of hand, with some taste for arrangement and effect. That was sufficient for the plaster decorations with which he was mainly occupied, and even for the little portraits in miniature or red chalk which he undertook. But he could not go beyond this, and the only attempt to paint an important picture which he made marks clearly the limits of his talent. His private life was somewhat irregular. He was a great lover of the fair sex, and towards the end of his life his wife was compelled to leave his home.

From the father, then, we may say, Ingres inherited the penetrating vivacity of his sight, the agile suppleness and surety of his fingers, and a certain voluptuous tendency which is particularly noticeable in his nudes; while his immense powers of work, his obstinacy and pugnacity, came from his mother.

At a very early age his father began to teach him drawing and music. He first achieved success as a violinist in the salon of the bishop, but he was at least equally precocious with his pencil. Towards the age of twelve he was taken to Toulouse. He was at first placed with the painter Vigan, and worked under his direction at the Académie Royale. Then he went to the atelier of Roques, where he made rapid progress. It was in Roques's studio that Ingres was converted to what he called "the religion of Raphael." Roques had brought back with him from Rome a number of copies of the works of the great painters of the Renaissance, among them one of Raphael's "Vierge à la Chaise." Ingres was so impressed by the beauty of this work that he is said to have burst into tears before it. The instruction at the Toulouse Academy, with its insistence on minute accuracy of drawing, also had a great influence on his future career. At the end of his life Ingres, when talking of his early studies at Toulouse, was fond of affirming that he was still "what the little Ingres of twelve years had been."

At the age of eighteen he was sent to Paris, and had the good fortune – it was his own expression – to be admitted to the studio of Louis David. He quickly gained the esteem of his master, and is said to have been employed to paint the accessories in David's famous portrait of Madame Récamier. But their good under-standing did not last long. Ingres competed for the Grand Prix de Rome in 1799, and David awarded the prize to Granger, an older pupil of his, while Ingres, to his great indignation, was only awarded the second prize. His picture was burnt during the Commune. The following year Ingres carried off the prize. The subject was "Achilles receiving in his Tent the Envoys of Agamemnon." Flaxman, the English sculptor and illustrator of Homer, spoke so flatteringly of Ingres' picture that, according to M. Delaborde, his master's hostility was still further increased. This painting, which is still preserved at the École des Beaux-Arts, shows the young man's power of vivid and accurate drawing and his respect for the teachings of his master. But under its external conformity to David's principles it is possible to trace the germs of an originality which was soon to separate the pupil, almost in spite of himself, from the school of his master. For while David admitted the direct imitation of nature only in his portraits and studies of the nude, he insisted on giving the first place to the search for the grand style in his historical compositions.

Already in this picture we see that Ingres was constitutionally incapable of sacrificing on any grounds his unconscious desire to imitate closely, of copying nature. In vain he tries to force himself to attain "style" in the group he has imagined. His group is not harmoniously arranged. It has no vital unity. Each of the figures appeared detached from the others; but they are drawn individually with so much realistic exactitude that the whole has the bizarre aspect of a photograph of an assembly of artists' models trying different poses in a studio.

As M. de Wyzewa has well said, the young painter had received from heaven at his birth a defect and a quality which remained intimately connected with each other. The defect was a total absence of imagination, invention, or aptitude to raise himself above the reality directly offered to the painter by the sight present to his eyes; and the quality – the very excess of which was the inevitable cause of the defect I have just denoted – the quality was a marvellous, an absolutely exceptional power of seeing, of understanding, and of reproducing that reality. No painter has ever had a more exact vision of the human figure, nor hands more skilful to fix in its entirety on the paper or the canvas what his eyes saw. A Holbein even, with all the fidelity of his realism, was still troubled in his observation of the model by a shade of æsthetic idealism, by the preoccupation of an example to be followed, or by a new process to employ: between Dominique Ingres and his model, so long as he had this model in front of his eyes, no consideration of any kind could interpose itself. The painter was as possessed by his vision, as hypnotised by it, and he was forced to copy it without changing anything. He carried away, indeed, as the result of his stay in David's studio, a body of doctrines to which he remained on the whole faithful all his life, but nature had given him gifts which were entirely different from those which were needed to put these doctrines into practice. And this explains why this great man, in the ignorance he always remained in of the real source of his originality and greatness, presents to us to-day the paradox of having been the most naturalistic of French painters, while obstinately attempting to make himself the most idealistic.

•

Having gained the much-coveted Prix de Rome, Ingres ought to have started at once for Italy. But the state of the public treasury was so miserable at this period of wars and internal crises that the young painter had to remain in Paris for five years before the funds for his journey were forthcoming. He was allotted apartments, together with other artists, in a deserted Capuchin convent in Paris, where he resumed his studies and undertook any work that was offered to him. The only official encouragement he received was an order to paint two portraits of Napoleon. The first of these portraits was finished in 1805 – the "Bonaparte, First Consul," for the town of Lille; the second, of "Napoleon, Emperor," for the Hôtel des Invalides, was finished in the following year. To those years of anxious suspense belong the first ideas of many of the works which were afterwards to make him famous. The dominant influences noticeable in his designs are said to be the works of Flaxman and the paintings on antique Greek vases. The neighbouring studio at the convent was occupied by de Gros, who was engaged upon a series of immense canvases consecrated to the glory of Napoleon's campaign in Egypt. It was filled with Oriental bric-à-brac, damascened arms, costumes, Persian rugs, Turkish pipes, and hangings of gold and silk – everything, in short, which would help the artist to paint the accessories of his pictures. It was in this studio that Ingres probably painted the studies of Eastern carpets, mosaics, &c., which are still preserved at the Museum of Montauban, and which he used afterwards in the "Odalisques." But the real strength of his personality is best seen in the series of portraits Ingres painted at this time. The first was a portrait of his father, who came to visit him in Paris in 1801. As was his custom, he worked on this in the following years, which explains the date, 1804, inscribed upon the painting. It was exhibited at the Salon in 1806, and is now at Montauban. Then he painted the portrait of himself which is now at the Museum of Chantilly. These were followed by the three portraits of the Rivière family, now in the Louvre. Two of these, those of the mother and daughter, have been reproduced in the present volume.

Towards the end of 1806 Ingres was at length supplied with the necessary funds to proceed to Rome. Once established in the Villa Medici fortune began to smile on him. He received several important official commissions. His talent also found private appreciators. The General Miollis, a fanatical admirer of Virgil; M. de Norvins, M. Marcotte; ladies like Madame de Lavalette, Madame Forgeot, and Madame Devauçay, gave him orders for portraits and pictures. Joachim Murat, then King of Naples, also took an interest in the young painter who had been born in the same province as himself. He commissioned the "Dormeuse de Naples" and the "Grande Odalisque," and invited him to his Court to paint portraits of the members of his family.

So flourishing did the young artist's affairs look that he resolved to face the responsibilities of marriage. He authorised a friend, a M. Loréal, an employé of the French Government in Rome, to find him a wife. M. Loréal's choice fell upon a Mlle. Magdaleine Chapelle, a young Frenchwoman of about the same age as the artist, who was then acting as cashier in a café at Guéret. M. Boyer d'Agen has recently published a letter from the young fiancée to her sister announcing the approaching marriage. It is dated 30th August 1813. She starts by saying that just as she was beginning to despair of ever finding a suitable husband "they had written to her from Rome saying they had found exactly what she wanted." "You can judge of the pleasure the news gave me," she exclaims quite frankly, "and it made me feel ten years younger, so that I now look only twenty years of age." She promises to send her sister a portrait of her future husband on another occasion, but says that for the present she must be satisfied with a verbal description. "He is a good-looking young man. I always said my husband must be handsome." "He is a painter – not a house-painter, but a great painter of history, a great talent. He earns from ten to twelve thousand livres a year. You see that with that we shall not die of hunger. He has a good character, and is very gentle. He is neither a drinker, a gambler, nor a rake. He has no faults. He promises to make me very happy, and I love to believe he will."

The writer of this charming letter was married to the artist about three months after it was written. The marriage was arranged entirely by the friends of the young couple. They had not set eyes on each other before Ingres went to the city gates to meet his affianced bride. They met near the Tomb of Nero. It was there that Ingres first took the hand of the partner who was to caress and console him during the next thirty-five years. This charming and laughing "fille à Madame Angot" turned out to be the admirable companion which every artist dreams of but so rarely possesses: one who will share all his hopes, but never his doubts; who believes and admires, smiles and is patient, and accepts all sacrifices for the glory of the one she loves.

Almost immediately after his marriage Ingres' luck changed. Murat was overthrown in 1814. His successor refused all the pictures that had been commissioned from Ingres, and those which had been finished were sold although the artist had not been paid for them. In a letter to his friend Gelibert, dated 7th July 1818, Ingres complains that he has been able to put nothing aside, that he has to live, as it were, from day to day. He admits he has several orders on hand for pictures, but "as I paint only to paint well, I take a long time over them, and consequently earn little." His chief resource was the making of chalk or pencil portraits, for which his usual price was twenty-five francs. But after each portrait, as his wife told a friend in after years, Ingres declared that he would not do any more, that he was a painter of history, not a draughtsman of the faces of the middle classes. "Nevertheless," she added, "it was necessary to live, and M. Ingres took up his pencil again." But as even this slender resource began to fail him at Rome, he resolved to leave that city and take up his residence at Florence, where his friend Bartolini, the sculptor, was already settled.

•

To this period of Ingres' first sojourn in Rome (from the end of

1806 to 1820) belong some of the artist's finest and most personal works. We must give the first place to his portraits. The delicious portrait of Madame Aymon, known as "La Belle Zélie" (now in the Museum of Rouen), was immediately followed by what is on all hands regarded as his most beautiful work of this kind. This is the "Madame Devauçay," of the Museum of Chantilly. It is an admirable example of Ingres' wonderful power of concentration and absorption in the thing seen. Disdaining the help of accessories, he draws all his inspiration from the face and figure of his model. He seizes the personality of his sitter with so much completeness and such perfect sympathy and understanding, and places it on the canvas with so much authority and power, that the portrait of the individual takes on all the scope of a permanent and absolute type. The portrait of "Madame de Sénonnes" (now in the Museum of Nantes), which was painted about 1810, has the same intensity of spirit as the "Madame Devauçay," and the same exquisite perfection of modelling and design. It is also marked by greater ease and freedom of handling, a sign of the young master's growing confidence in his own genius. It is generally regarded as Ingres' masterpiece of feminine portraiture.

The well-known "Œdipus and the Sphinx" was painted in 1808, while the artist was still a pensioner of the School of Rome. It is hard for us to understand the horror and dislike which this picture provoked among the leading spirits of the school of David. What seems to us a typical example of classic art struck the official representatives of Classicism as the work of a revolutionary. In his report on this picture, M. Lethière, the director of the School of Rome, regrets that M. Ingres, in spite of his talent, has failed to grasp the secret of the "grand and noble style of the great masters of the Roman school." To appreciate the originality and daring of this work, we must compare the figure of Œdipus with that of the Roman heroes in David's "Rape of the Sabines." David's figures are all cast in the same mould. All the particularities of the individual model are ruthlessly eliminated. When we turn from the vague and empty generalisations of David, Regnault, Gérard and Girodet, and look at the narrow forehead, the pugnacious upper lip, the prominent cheek-bones, the deep-sunk eye and the bushy eyebrows of Ingres' figure, we may begin to understand that the gulf which yawns between the two kinds of Idealism – the abstract idealism of the Davidian school and the concrete idealism of Ingres – is quite as wide and impassable as that which separates them both from Romanticism and Naturalism.

•

The "Œdipus" was followed, in 1808, by the "Seated Bather" (now in the Louvre); in 1811, by "Jupiter and Thétis" (now at the Museum of Aix), a curiously Flaxman-like design; in 1812, by the "Dream of Ossian" (now at Montauban); and in 1814, by a scene of real life, "The Pope officiating among the Cardinals in the Sistine Chapel" (now in the Louvre). In this marvellous picture the artist has for once avoided the painful task of invention which he habitually imposed upon himself. He abandoned himself completely to the imperious suggestion of what was actually before his eyes. The truth, life, and richness of colour and tone of this little picture have led some of his recent admirers to speak of it as the most complete and perfectly balanced of all the artist's works.

The "Grande Odalisque," exhibited at the Salon of 1819, but painted in 1814, brought to a close for the time the admirable series of nude female figures which the artist had begun during his first years in Rome. His wonderful sketches of the "Venus Anadyomene" and the "Source" had already been painted, but the canvases remained unfinished in his studio, the first till 1848, the second till 1858.

His love of female beauty reveals itself again in the principal figure of the picture he sent to the Salon in 1819. This was the "Roger delivering Angelica," a scene borrowed from the tenth song of Ariosto's "Roland Furieux." The picture is now in the Louvre. The young knight, mounted on a hippogriff, pierces with his lance a marine monster who was about to devour the beautiful young woman who is chained to the rocks. The figure of the young knight, his curious steed, and the strange monster which is being killed, provoked the anger and ridicule of the Academic party. In its quaint details the influence of Perugino and of the earlier Florentine and Tuscan painters was clearly noticeable. This was one of the first signs in nineteenth-century art of the Gothic revival and of that stream of tendency which came afterwards to be described as pre-Raphaelitism. The epithet "Gothic" was freely used as a term of reproach against Ingres' picture. But the lovely figure of Angelica was a distinct creation of the painter's own genius.

In the "Francesca da Rimini" of the same year (now in the Museum of Angers) the same pre-Raphaelite tendencies are even more strongly pronounced. The figures of the two lovers might easily have been designed by Rossetti or Maddox Brown.

•

All these works in which the master's genius had approved itself with so much originality and fire had left their author to vegetate in poverty and obscurity, while the mediocrities around him had risen rapidly towards fortune and celebrity. Ingres was now anxious to return to Paris, but his meagre resources would not allow it. Then, tired of his hardships, and feeling that the social atmosphere of Rome was not favourable to him, he rejoined his friend Bartolini at Florence, hoping thus, among new surroundings, to re-establish his compromised career. His hopes were falsified. The four years passed in Florence (1820-1824) brought him only a fresh supply of hardships and mortifications. Less hospitable than Rome, Florence brought him only two commissions for portraits, those of M. and Mme. Leblanc (1823-1824); but it was here that he met M. de Pastoret, who was instrumental in getting him the commission which brought the artist his first striking and definitive success. M. de Pastoret was so pleased with Ingres' "Entry of Charles V. into Paris" (painted in 1821) that he obtained for him a commission from the Minister of the Interior for a large picture of "The Vow of Louis XIII." for the Cathedral of Montauban. This was begun in Florence in 1821 and finished in 1824, in which year it figured in the Salon of Paris. It was one of his pictures with which Ingres was most satisfied. It is also one of the first in which the influence of Raphael, which was to play such a large part in all his future work, is conspicuous. In a letter written in 1821, Ingres said that he was sparing no pains to make the picture "Raphaelesque and his own." There is really more of Raphael in it than Ingres. The general arrangement of the design reminds one at once of Raphael's "Transfiguration," "The Sistine Madonna," and the "Mass of Bolsena." The figure of the Madonna is a sort of amalgam of Raphael's various Madonnas. There is also an evident want of faith and religious enthusiasm in the picture. It marked the subjection of the artist to the Academical party which he had fought till then with so much violence and bitterness. The public which had frowned upon his vigorously personal and original works hailed this able imitation with enthusiasm. The master's period of probation was at an end, and he returned in triumph to Paris to become the leader of the Academic party against the rising tide of Romanticism.

Ingres' life was henceforward free from the material cares which had hampered his early career. The Parisians declared that such a picture as the "Vow of Louis XIII." was too good to be buried in the provinces. The State wanted to retain it for Notre Dame or Val-de-Grace, and offered the artist a much larger sum of money for it than had been agreed upon. But Ingres refused these flattering offers. He was determined that Montauban should have it as an offering of his filial affection. The picture was taken there from Paris. The artist was entertained at a banquet given by the Municipality. Flattering speeches were made, and the artist departed with the cheers of his admirers ringing in his ears. And then the Archbishop, objecting to the nakedness of the infant Jesus and the two amorini holding the tablet, refused to permit the picture to be brought into the Cathedral. The artist's friends were indignant; Ingres himself was furious. But prayers and threats could not move the Archbishop. It was only when large gilt fig-leaves had been placed to cover up the innocent nakedness of the charming little figures that he would allow the canvas to be hung in his church.

In 1824 Ingres was nominated Chevalier of the Legion of Honour. In 1825 he was elected to the Institute. Charles X. com missioned him to paint his portrait in the royal robes, and to decorate one of the ceilings of the Louvre. At the end of 1829 he was made professor at the École des Beaux-arts.

•

"The Apotheosis of Homer," the subject chosen for the Louvre ceiling, was begun and finished within the short space of a single year. The amount of work involved in making the preparatory studies and carrying through a work of such importance was enormous, and Ingres had never before displayed so much energy and decision. The conception of the picture was a noble one. It was to represent the spiritual ties which bind one generation of human beings to the other; to insist on the debt which each worker in the field of art and thought owes to his predecessors; to celebrate the real immortality of genius by showing the incessant action which it exerts on all the individuals who are successively born and developed by its influence. We must confess that Ingres has found a worthy plastic formula to express his highly abstract conception. He shows us the poets, painters, sculptors, philosophers, and great patrons of the arts grouped round the seat of the old blind poet. Each individual face, each gesture and pose, has been studied and thought out patiently, and executed with masterly skill. The terrible problem of grouping together so many different personalities and so many costumes of widely differing periods has been faced and overcome. The whole produces an effect of incomparable simplicity and grandeur.

In no part of the pictures are Ingres' marvellous powers of realisation more clearly displayed than in the three purely symbolical figures of the Winged Victory who places the crown of gold upon the forehead of the poet, and those representing the *Odyssey* and the *Iliad* who sit at his feet. What a distance separates these figures, full of feminine charm and of exuberant life, from the cold allegories of the other painters of his time! Look at the queenly grace of the Victory; the disdainful lips, the contracted nostrils of the proud woman, with hands nervously crossed upon her knee, who sits on the poet's right; and the dreamer who sits on his left, with her mantle wrapped round her, her hand upon her chin, her half-closed eyes dreaming of the far-away adventures of Ulysses.

This picture remained in the place for which it was destined for about twenty years. Then it was replaced by an excellent copy made by three of the master's pupils, Dumas and the brothers Baize, and the original was hung in the Louvre, where it could be better seen and admired by the public and more carefully studied by the painters.

Such a display of his powers disarmed even the many enemies which Ingres had made. But the artist was never satisfied. He thought he had not attained the supreme and definitive expression of his genius. He thought he could do better, that he could express himself with more force, more persuasive energy and warmth, in his next work. This was a religious scene commissioned for the Cathedral of Autun – the "Martyrdom of St. Symphorian."

Before this work was finished he painted yet another of those superb portraits which he himself professed to regard as a waste of time, but which posterity values more highly than the allegorical and religious subjects to which he devoted himself with such fierce energy and consuming ardour. This was the portrait of "Bertin ainé," which was exhibited at the Salon of 1833, and is now in the Louvre. The old man, with turbulent grey hair, with keen penetrating eyes, with wary mouth, seated so squarely in his chair with his hands on his knees – the whole bodily and spiritual presence of the man is placed so vividly upon the canvas that we seem to know him more intimately than we know our friends.

After being repainted several times, the "Martyrdom of St

Symphorian" was exhibited at the Salon the year after the portrait of M. Bertin had appeared there. Instead of bringing Ingres a more complete victory than his "Homer," it brought him an unexpected check. To us, living as we do in a perfect anarchy of taste, it is rather difficult to understand why this picture should have scandalised and alarmed the artists and public of the time. The artist was accused of exaggeration, of an abuse of power. Since Michelangelo they had never seen in painting such muscles as those of the arms and legs of the lictors who are taking the saint to his place of torture. The whole effect, Ingres' critics said, was forced and improbable. They did not understand that the artist had deliberately intended to force the contrast between the bestiality of the murderers and the moral superiority of their victim.

In spite of its want of atmosphere and other shortcomings, the picture is a moving and impressive one. There is nothing vulgar in those too robust figures. The face of the young martyr, illuminated with faith, and the fanatical exaltation of the mother, form the two moral centres of the drama. Between them the curiosity and emotion of the crowd are divided. Some gaze in stupor at this woman who sends her son to torture. They do not understand that she sees him already in glory, crowned with celestial beatitudes. Others are indignant with her, like the young man who picks up a stone to throw at her, or like the soldier behind the centurion who turns towards her a face full of astonishment and irritation. A young woman presses her child in her arms in shuddering protestation. Others look at the man who is about to die for his faith. Their sentiments oscillate between hostility, compassion, indifference, and horror. The women are grieved. An old man takes his head in his hands, confounded by such inconceivable folly. And, dominating them all, the centurion on horseback gives the order to march to the place of execution.

The learned construction of such a crowded scene, the nobility and expressiveness of the figures, the fine treatment of drapery, the virile energy of the drawing, the sober and restrained colouring, and, above all, that indefinable beauty which genius stamps on all its creations, might well have silenced the adverse criticisms with which the artists and the public assailed this picture.

Ingres suffered from these criticisms to a quite unreasonable extent. "I do not belong to this apostate century," he exclaimed. He could not understand people's objections, nothing could console him, and he cursed his epoch and the injustice of the public. He swore he would never exhibit at the Salon again. He wished to flee from Paris. He accepted as a deliverance the appointment of Director of the Academy of France in Rome, shut his studio, dismissed his pupils, and with an indignant and bitter spirit he quitted Paris again for the Eternal City.

•

But if Ingres doubted of human justice, he never doubted about his art. He devoted himself to it with renewed passion and enthusiasm. "The day I quitted Paris," he wrote to one of his friends, "I broke for ever with everything that has to do with the public. Henceforth I will paint entirely for myself. I belong at last to myself, and I will belong only to myself."

But, as a fact, neither Ingres' influence nor prestige suffered from the want of success of his "St. Symphorian." As director of the French Academy at Rome he remained the guide, counsellor, and example of all the young talents of his time. His proud ideal could not fail to attract the enthusiasm of his younger contemporaries. His teaching and example were helpful to others besides the painters. What was essential in his doctrines was applicable to all the arts: to music, which moved him so profoundly; and to sculpture – for did he not use his pencil and brush like a chisel?

Official favour also followed him in his angry retreat. The Duke of Orleans ordered a small historical picture from him, which gave him an immense deal of trouble but was at the same time a source of glorious compensation. He produced "Stratonice," one of the most successful of his works.

The tragedy of which Stratonice was the heroine had haunted his imagination for years. He had meditated long on the subject, but had always conceived the picture on a large scale. Unfortunately, the picture had to be the same size as Paul Delaroche's "Death of the Duke of Guise," to which it was to serve as pendant, and Ingres was constrained to transform his grandiose conception into a miniature. Ingres took six years to paint what he called his "grand historical miniature." And it is to be somewhat regretted that in his anxiety for archæological exactitude he invited the collaboration of the architect Hittorf. Hittorf was full of his rather excessive theories about the polychromatic architecture of the ancients. He imposed his ideas so completely on the unfortunate artist that he was permitted to paint the background of the picture. Hence the debauch of local colour, of coloured mosaics and bronzes, which threatens almost to swamp the figures. And what is worse, later archæologists have not failed to discover flaws in the pedantic architect's too insistent details – strange anachronisms like that of placing well-known Pompeiian frescoes on the walls of the palace of Antiochus, together with motives borrowed from Greek vases at least four hundred years earlier in date. The example of this picture has had an important effect on the French school.

But in spite of these defects, the picture imposes itself on the imagination. The hopeless tragedy of the situation is admirably expressed without a trace of theatrical exaggeration. We see a young man, suffering from a grave and mysterious malady, extended upon his bed of suffering. The physician called in by his despairing father stands beside him and examines him. The father himself, overcome with grief, bows his head over his son's couch. At this moment in the chamber of death a young woman enters. She is young, charming, and melancholy. She is the second wife of the heart-broken father, the mother-in-law of the dying son. And as she walks through the room with languishing steps the physician guesses the horrible truth. The man on the bed is dying of love. By signs which cannot deceive him, the man of science has divined the dreadful passion of the son for his father's wife. Such was, in fact, the history of Stratonice. The second wife of Seleucus Nicanor was loved by Antiochus, the king's son by his first marriage. The doctor, Erasistratus, having surprised this secret, declared that the young man would certainly die if Stratonice was not given to him, and his father's love was great enough to enable him to make this sacrifice.

No other artist than Ingres could have placed this poignant drama on canvas without exciting ridicule. "Stratonice" was exhibited by the Duke of Orleans in one of the galleries of the Pavilion of Marsan, and the public were freely admitted to see it. All the visitors were enchanted with it. The dramatic character of the subject was not displeasing to the Parisian public, and the artists admired the delicate taste, the pathetic grace, and the impeccable style of the workmanship. Above all, the charm of the *svelte* and supple figure of the heroine, her head bowed under the weight of her culpable beauty, touched all hearts.

Another small picture, known indifferently as "The Odalisque with the Slave" or the "Small Odalisque," was finished about the same time as the "Stratonice." This was painted for the artist's friend M. Marcotte, but is now in the Louvre. In the "Odalisque" as in the "Stratonice" we find a profusion of the details dear to Hittorf, but the figure of the beautiful Circassian curled up on the rich carpet of the harem is a masterpiece of plastic form. In this lovely body the artist has symbolised something of that perverse melancholy, that dangerous voluptuousness, which has found such moving expression in some of Baudelaire's poems.

•

In the spring of 1841 Ingres returned to Paris. He found his reputation increased by the success of the "Stratonice." His brother artists hailed him as their leader. A banquet was offered to him by all the artists present in the capital, painters, sculptors, and architects, the only prominent absentee being Eugène Delacroix, the leader of the Romantics. Delacroix did not wish to participate in the triumph of his rival, and this triumph, so unanimously accorded, only served to widen the breach between the two masters. Henceforth the struggle between them became more bitter. Each party pursued the other without mercy, neither disdaining to use any kind of weapon that came to hand.

Fortified by the homage offered to him, Ingres returned to his work with renewed ardour. The King asked him to paint a portrait of the Duke of Orleans, and Ingres, grateful for the Duke's kindness with regard to the "Stratonice," took much more pains over this portrait than he usually took with commissions of this kind. This was the last male portrait that Ingres painted, with the exception of a small monochrome medallion of the Prince Jéròme Napoléon, which he executed in 1855. But, on the other hand, he became the favourite painter of the exalted dames of the Monarchy of July and of the Second Empire, though very much against his will, for he regarded portrait-painting as a waste of time, and wished to devote himself entirely to his grand historical and religious compositions. Nevertheless, he painted some fine portraits of beautiful women – Madame d'Haussonville in 1845, Madame Frédéric Reisat in 1846, Madame James de Rothschild in 1848, Madame Gonse and Madame Moitessier in 1852, the Princess de Broglie in 1853, a second half-length portrait (the first was a full-length) of Madame Moitessier in 1856, and finally, in 1859, that of his second wife.

•

Soon after the portrait of the Duke of Orleans was finished he received another royal commission, the "Jesus among the Doctors," which the Queen Marie-Amélie wished to present to the Château de Bizy. The work, badly conceived at the beginning, was still unfinished when the Revolution drove from France the patroness who had commissioned it. It remained almost forgotten in a corner of the artist's studio till 1862, when Ingres decided to finish it and present it to the museum of his natal city. Of all Ingres' productions, it is perhaps the only one where the inspiration and execution both seem feeble.

While he had been still in Rome, in 1839, Ingres had received from the Duc de Luynes a commission to decorate the great room at the Château of Dampierre with two large mural paintings representing "The Age of Gold" and "The Age of Iron." He was delighted with the commission, as he was always dreaming of reviving the great traditions of decorative painting. He made numberless studies for these subjects, many of them among the most beautiful of his drawings. But as the painting had to be done actually on the walls at Dampierre, the work progressed very slowly. Years flew by, and the artist's enthusiasm cooled. The noble Duke and the sensitive and proud painter could not get along well under the same roof. Ingres thought himself slighted on one occasion (in 1850) and brusquely threw up the commission, leaving his work unfinished. There exists of this gigantic work only a sketch at Dampierre, an infinite number of drawings at the Museum of Montauban, and a little painting executed from these drawings in 1862, a very feeble representation of what the definitive work would have been. As for "The Age of Iron," we have only the preliminary studies.

•

As if to revenge himself for the loss of his promised masterpiece, Ingres now took up again a number of the works he had sketched in his youth and set himself to finish them or repaint them. He also busied himself painting replicas of others which had passed out of his hands but with which he was not entirely satisfied. He painted thus a repetition of the "Apotheosis of Homer," adding a number of fresh figures and substituting others for some of the poets and artists of his first choice. After much anxious reflection and discussion with his pupils, he decided to banish Shakespeare, as he had already banished Goethe, from the group of the immortals. He also painted replicas of his "Sistine Chapel," of "Roger delivering Angelica," and variations of his "Œdipus" and "Stratonice." He also painted four or five slightly different versions of the figure of the Virgin in his early picture of the "Vow of Louis XIII." One of these developed into a picture of "The Virgin between St. Nicholas and St.

Alexander" – a subject the Emperor of Russia had asked him to treat. We find another version of the same type in "The Virgin with the Host," which forms one of our illustrations. In no other work of Ingres is his passionate admiration of Raphael more clearly displayed.

One of the new works which caused the liveliest sensation was "The Birth of Venus" or "Venus Anadyomene." This had been begun forty years before, at the time of the early "Bathers" and "Odalisque." The beautiful white body of the goddess detaches itself from the harmonious blue of the sea and sky, and groups of amorini flutter round and caress her youthful form. One of these delicious attendants offers her a mirror, another kisses the feet of the young goddess, while a third embraces her knees. It would be difficult to imagine anything more graciously tender or more natural than the infantile figures.

The "Venus Anadyomene" was finished in 1848; in 1851 Ingres painted his "Jupiter and Antiope," and two years later he painted his "Apotheosis of Napoleon I.," a large subject for the decoration of one of the ceilings of the Hôtel de Ville, at Paris. This was unfortunately destroyed by fire in the troubled days of the Commune in 1871. In 1854 his "Joan of Arc assisting at the Consecration of Charles VII." was painted for the gallery of Versailles.

We have now reached the last years of the artist's laborious life. They were as busy as his earlier years, but they were crowned with honour and glory. In 1855 all Europe flocked to Paris to see the Universal Exhibition. The life-work of Ingres was gathered together in a special gallery. It produced an immense impression. All criticisms of detail fell before the magnificent affirmation of the artist's individual ideal. One of the grand medals was given to him by the unanimous votes of the artists, and the Emperor made him an officer of the Legion of Honour.

Then, in the following year, as if to crown his career by the evocation of a supreme masterpiece, Ingres finished the "Source," a subject which had been begun at the same time as the "Venus

Anadyomene." This beautiful figure was not a passing vision which had animated the brush of the aged painter; it was indeed the daughter of his dreams, an emanation of his own soul, the slow growth of long meditations, and which, at last, incarnated itself in an immortal form. This calm and adorable figure seems a souvenir of our long-lost innocence. That is perhaps why we love it so, and why we bless the artist to whom we owe this divine dream.

Ingres died in 1867. He had finished his task, had spoken the last word of his austere but profoundly human genius.

•

Ingres has been spoken of as an ancient Greek lost and bewildered in our modern times. Such a view of his character is misleading. Like all the great creators, he expressed the aspirations of his race and his times. He was not only the child of his century and his country, but he represented them both in their classic reaction and in their impulse towards Romanticism. But the two tendencies were so nicely balanced in his temperament that he offended the extremists of both parties. He paid in his lifetime for his detachment from parties, for his exalted aims and sublime courage, but he reaps his reward from posterity. The creator of the immortal figures of Œdipus, the Odalisque, Angelica, Stratonice, and the Source to-day takes unquestioned rank among the great masters not only of French but of European art.

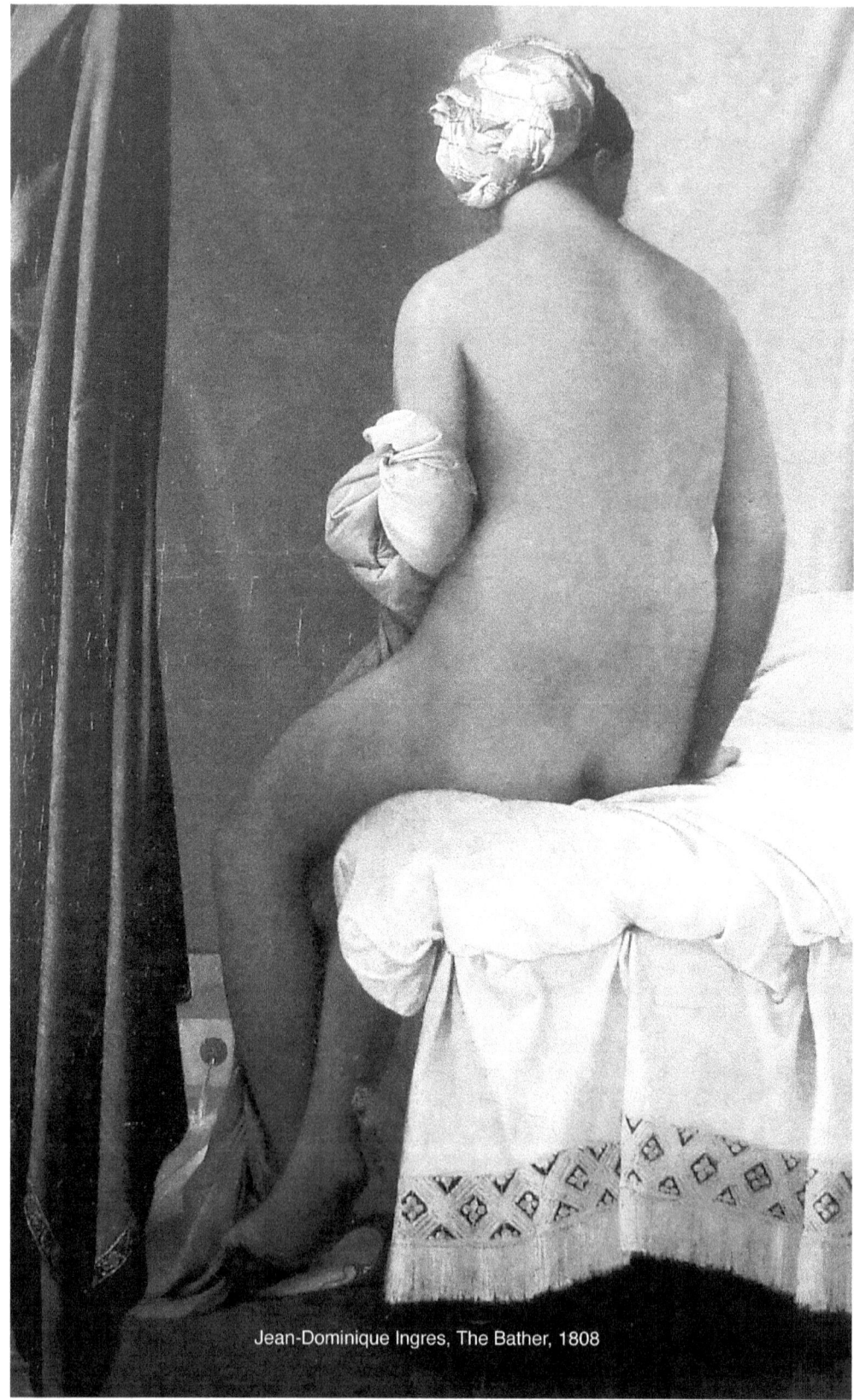

Jean-Dominique Ingres, The Bather, 1808

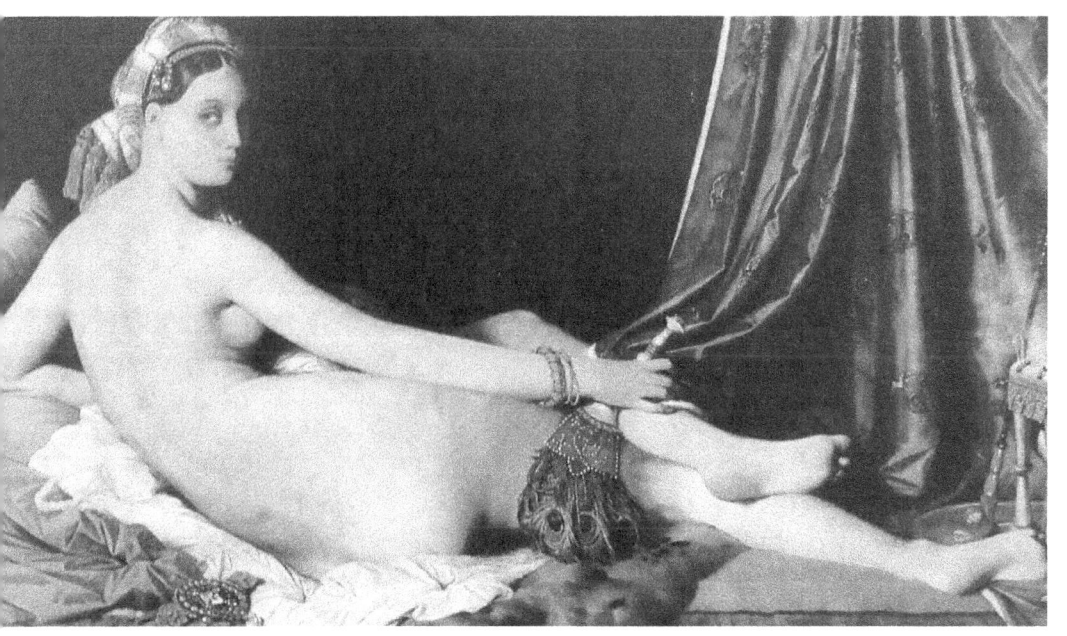

Jean-Dominique Ingres, Grand Odalisque, 1814

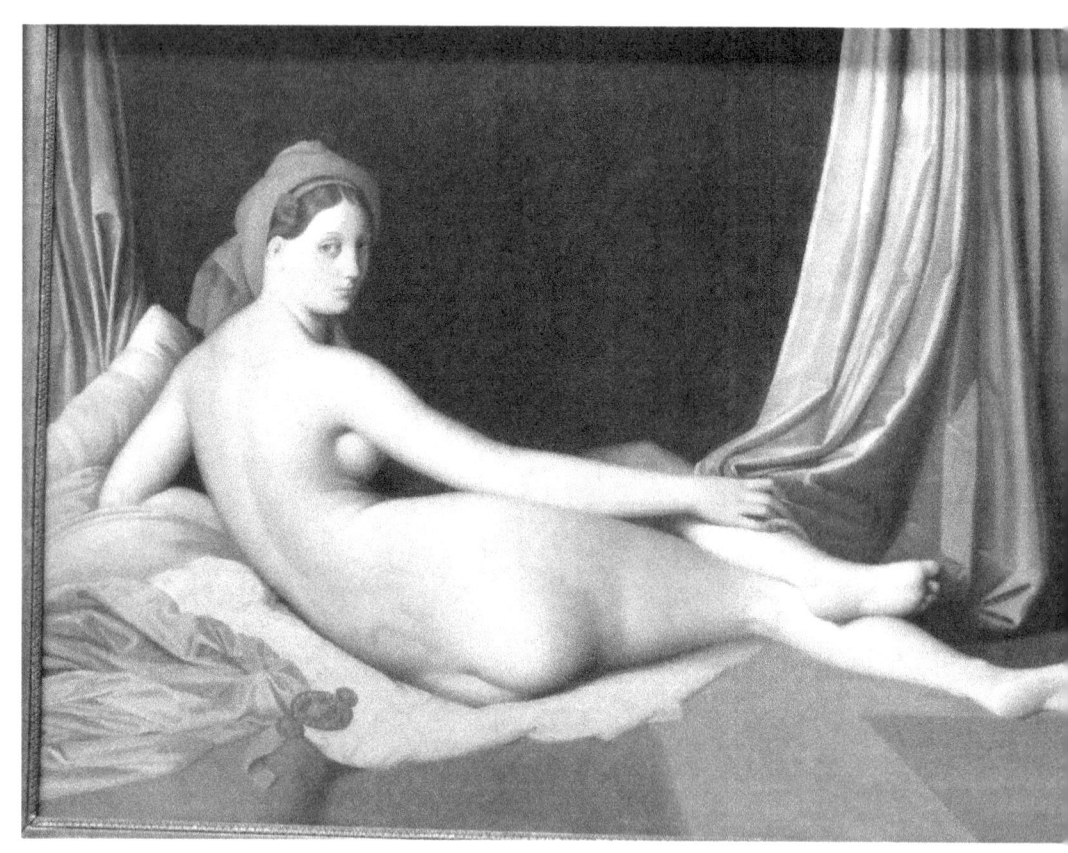

J.A.D. Ingres, Odalisque, Metropolitan Museum of Art

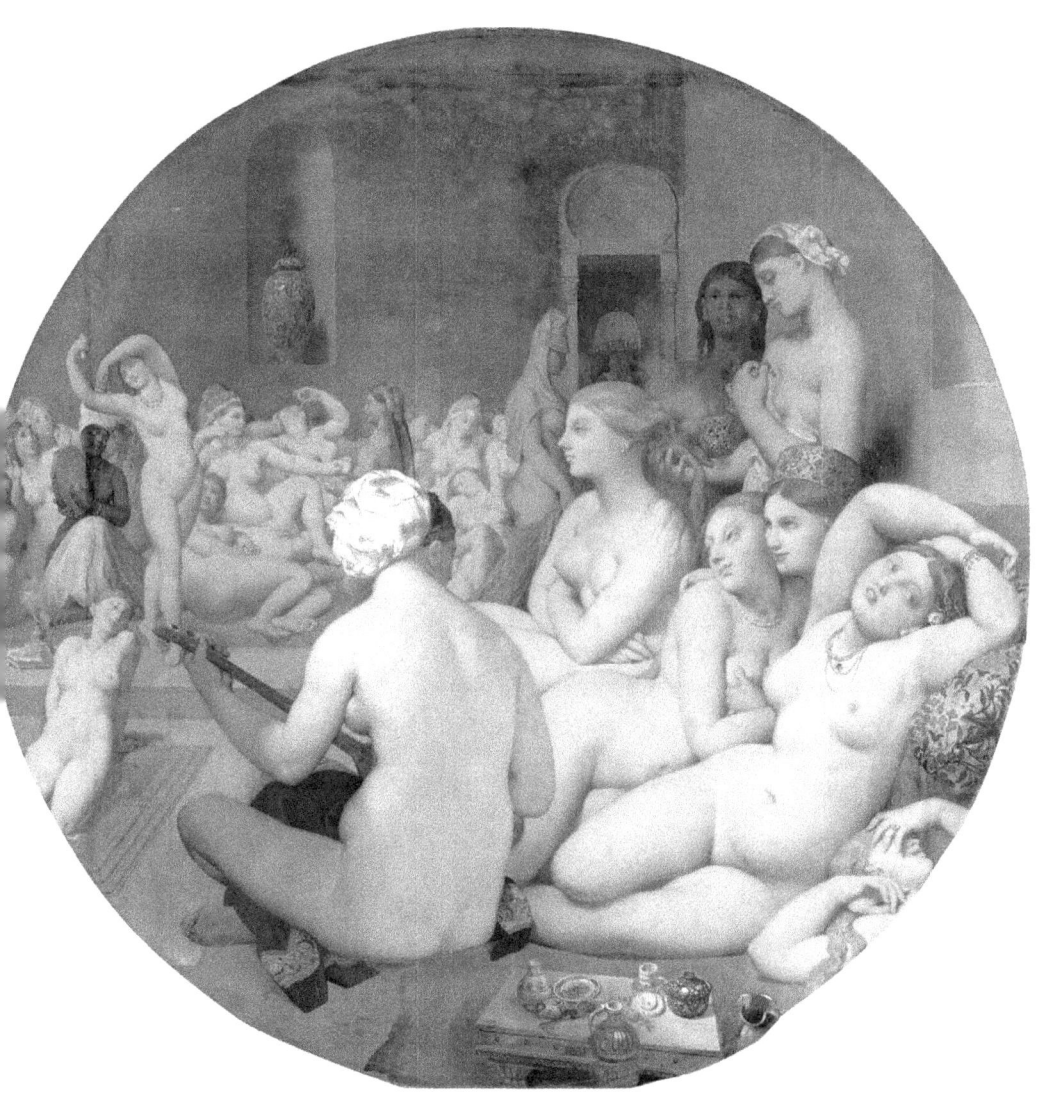

J.A.D. Ingres, Turkish Bath, 1862, Louvre

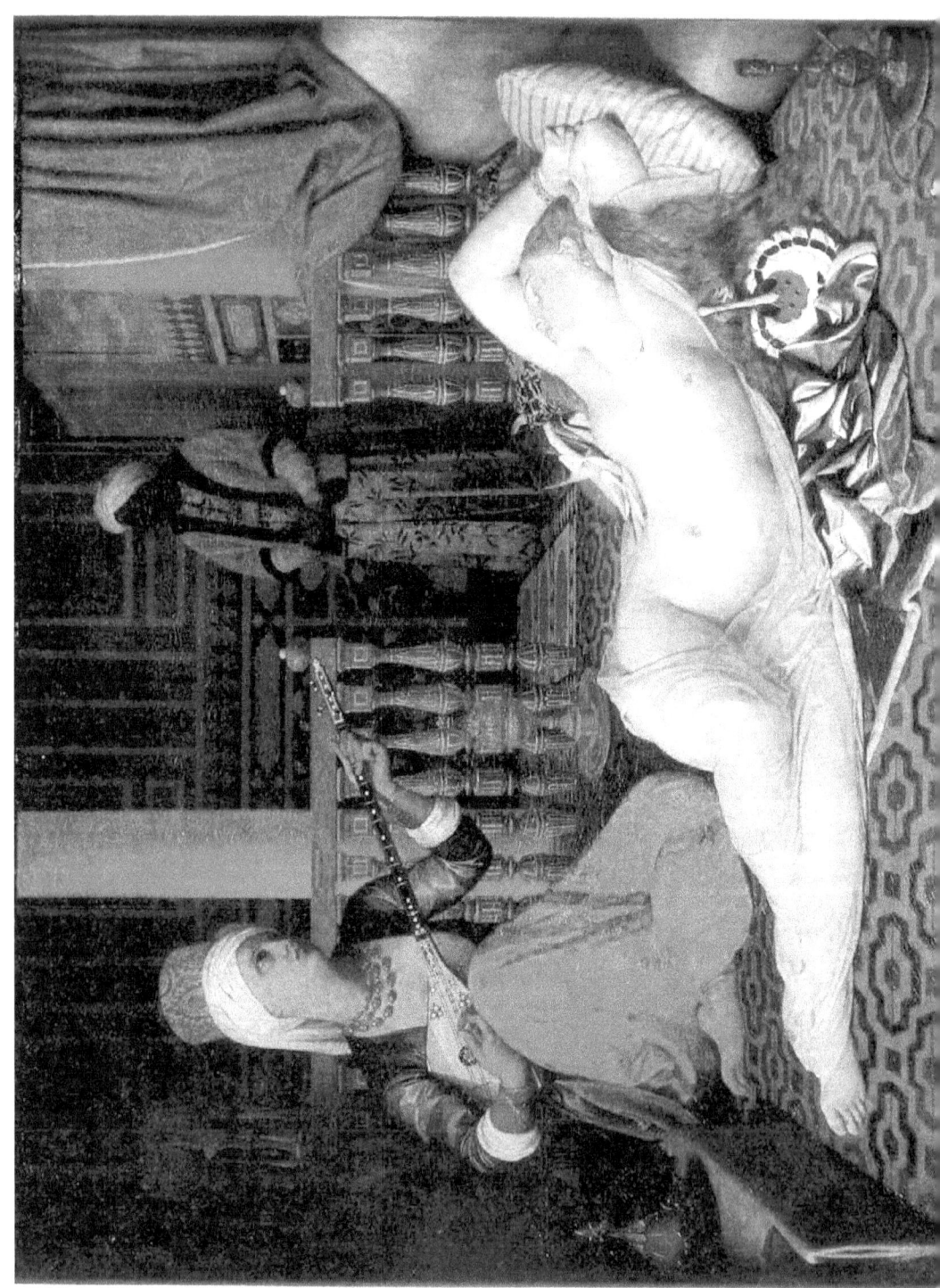

Jean-Dominique Ingres, Odalisque

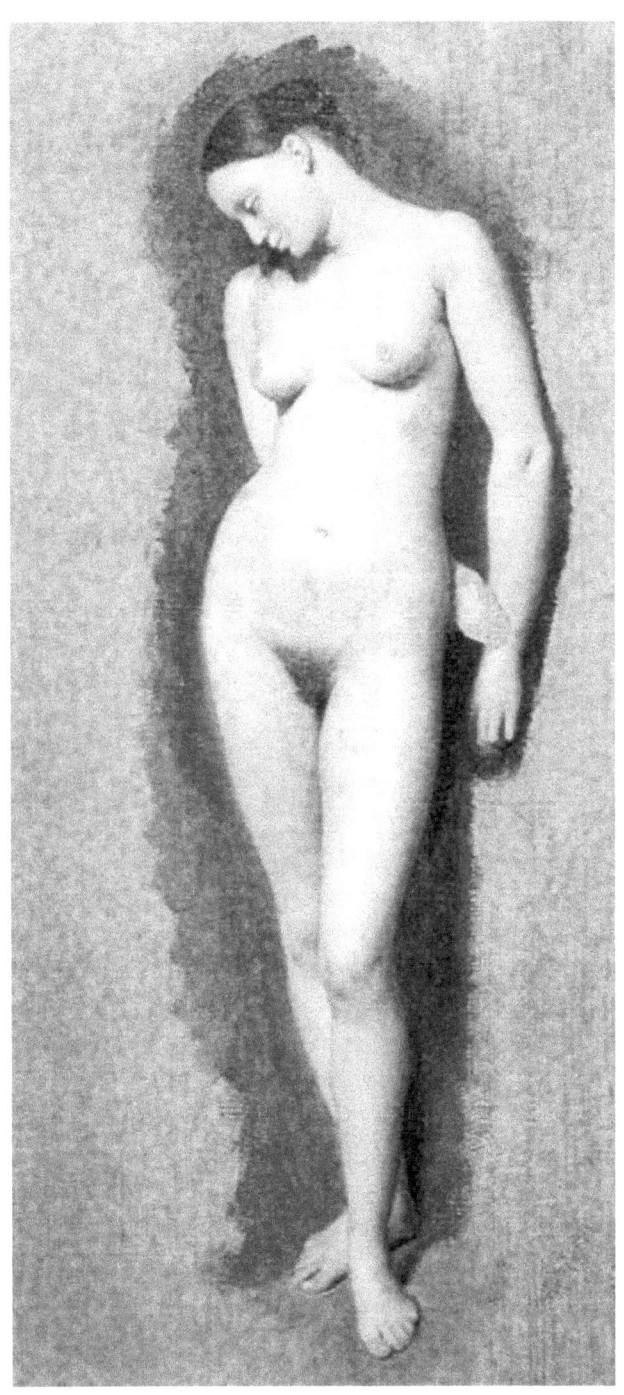

Jean-Dominique Ingres, Nude Study

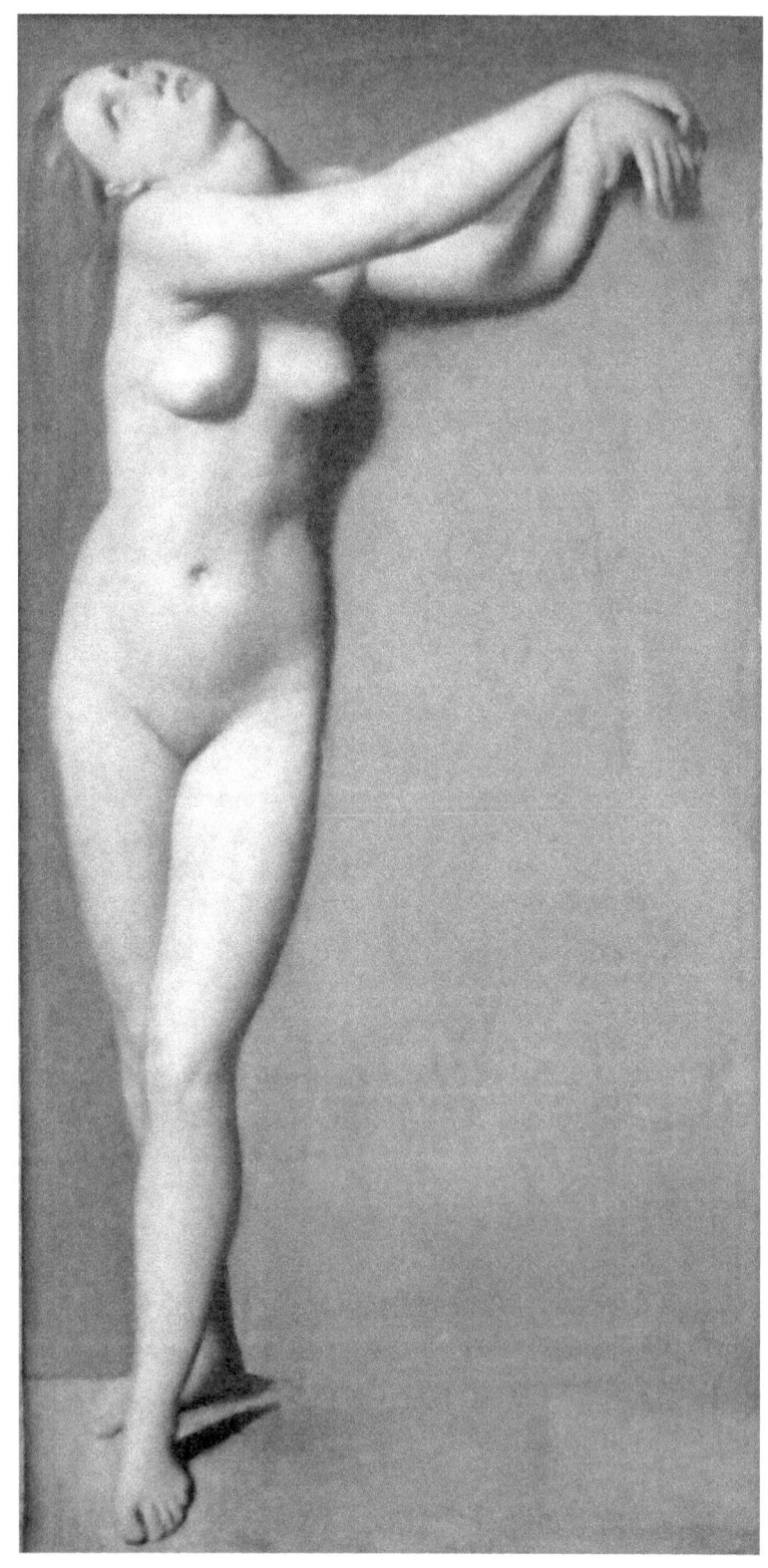

J.A.D. Ingres, study for Ruggiero

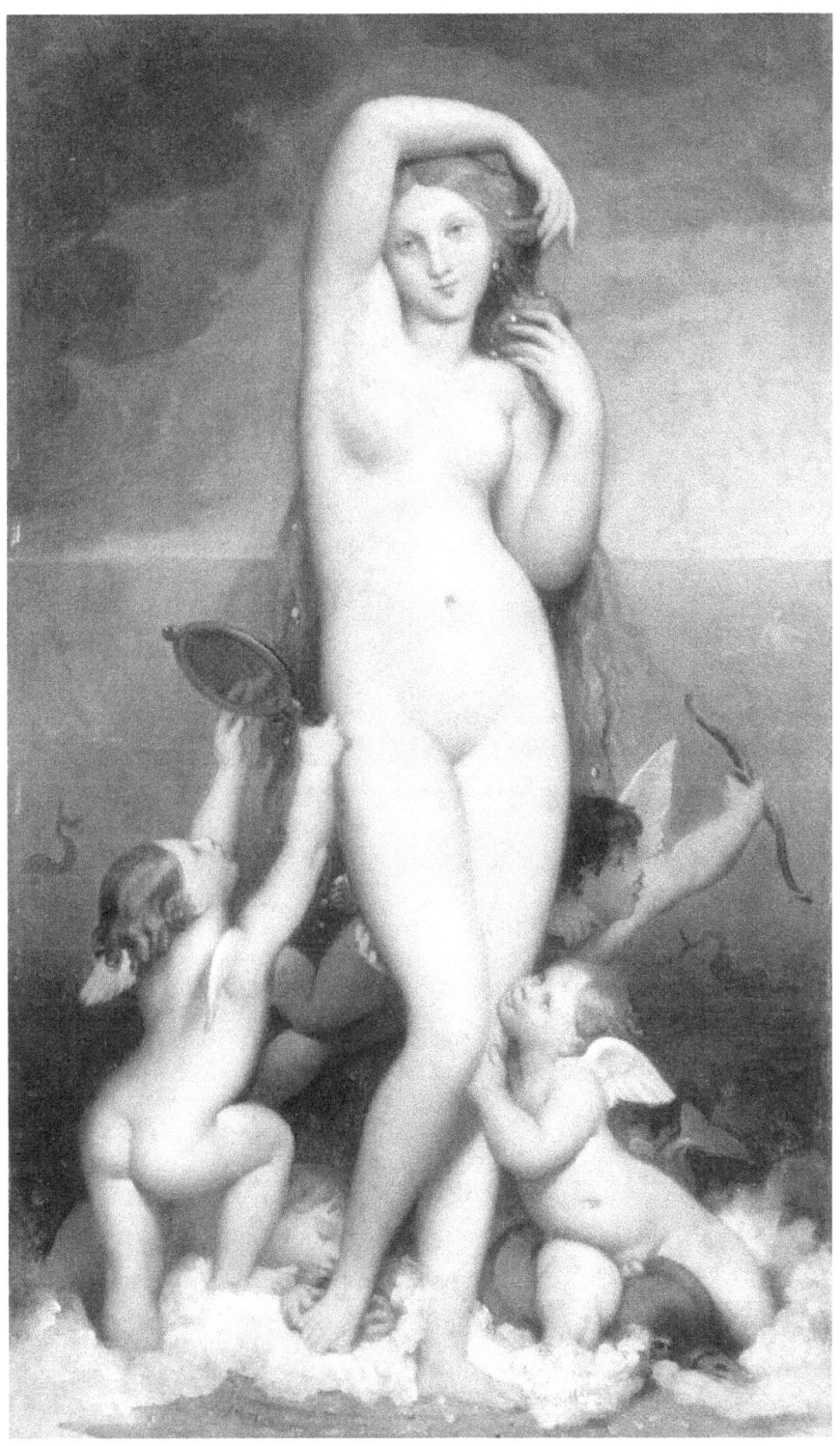

J.A.D. Ingres, Venus Anadyomène, 1825-50, Paris

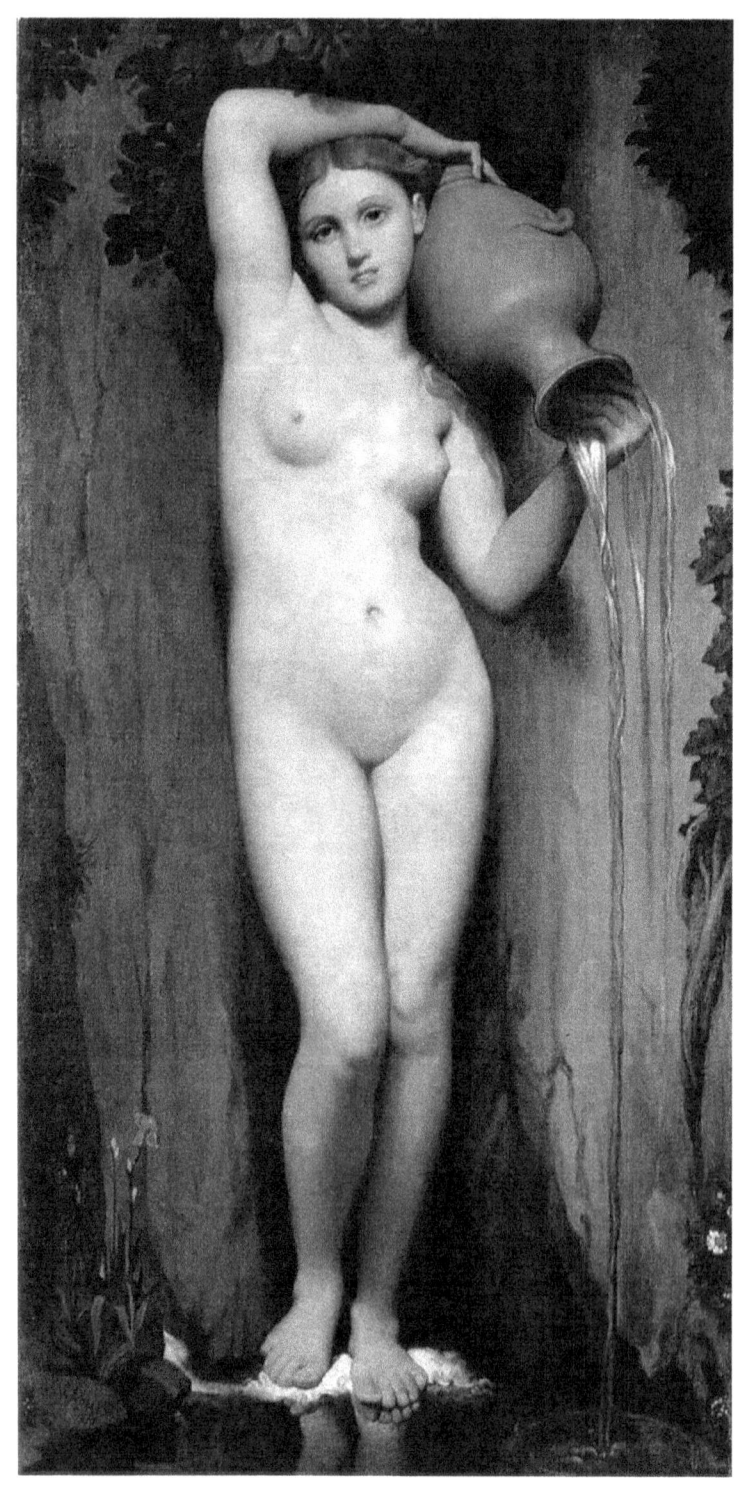

J.A.D.Ingres, The Source, 1856, Paris

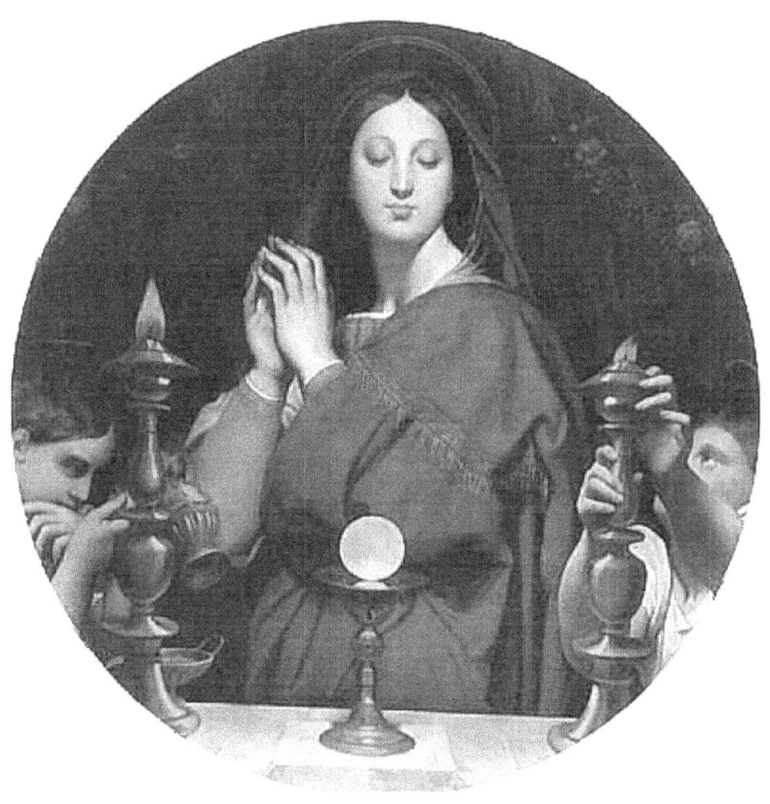

J.A.D. Ingres, The Virgin of the Host, 1852,
Metropolitan Museum of Art

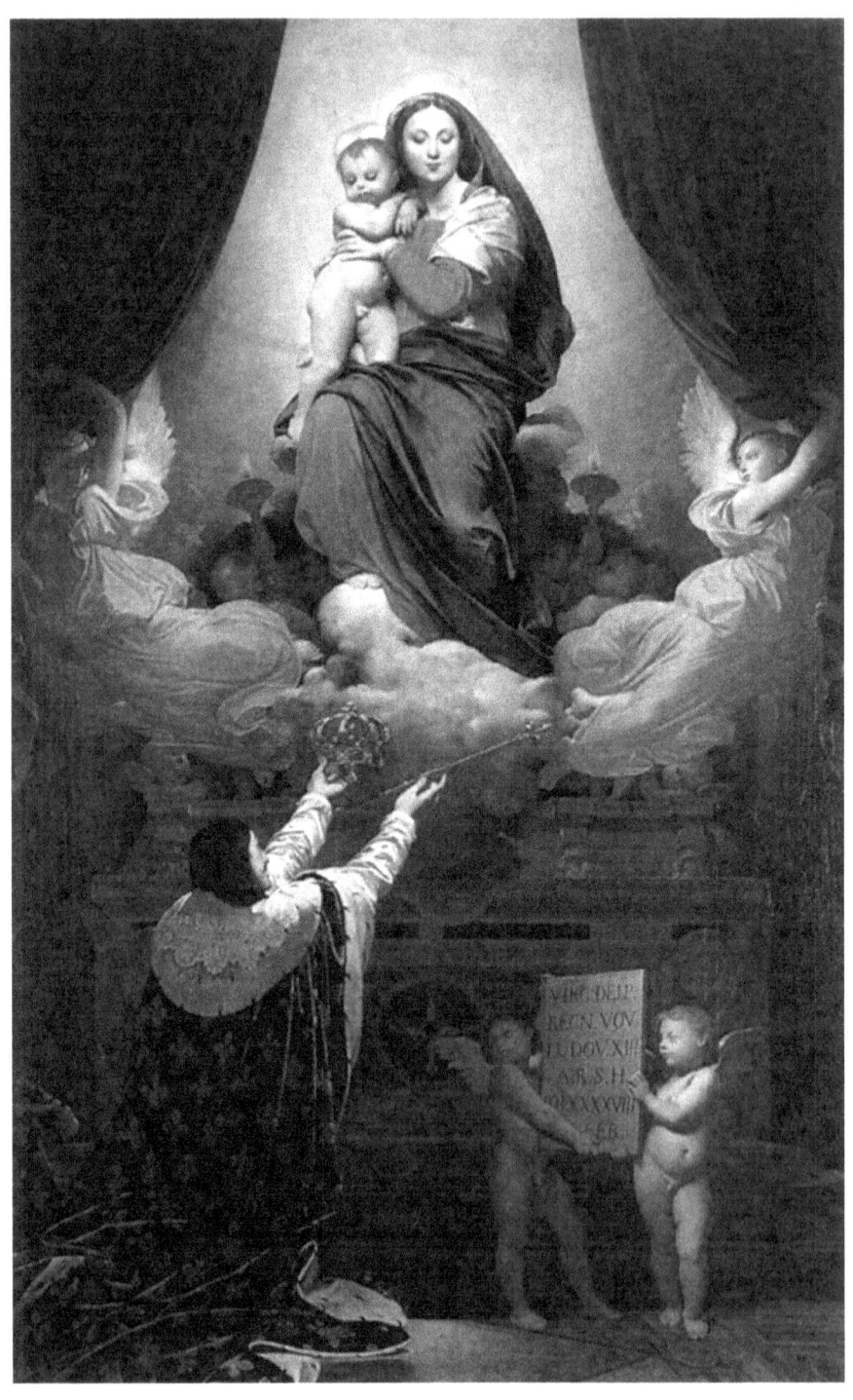

J.A.D. Ingres, O Voto de Luis XIII, 1824, Montauban

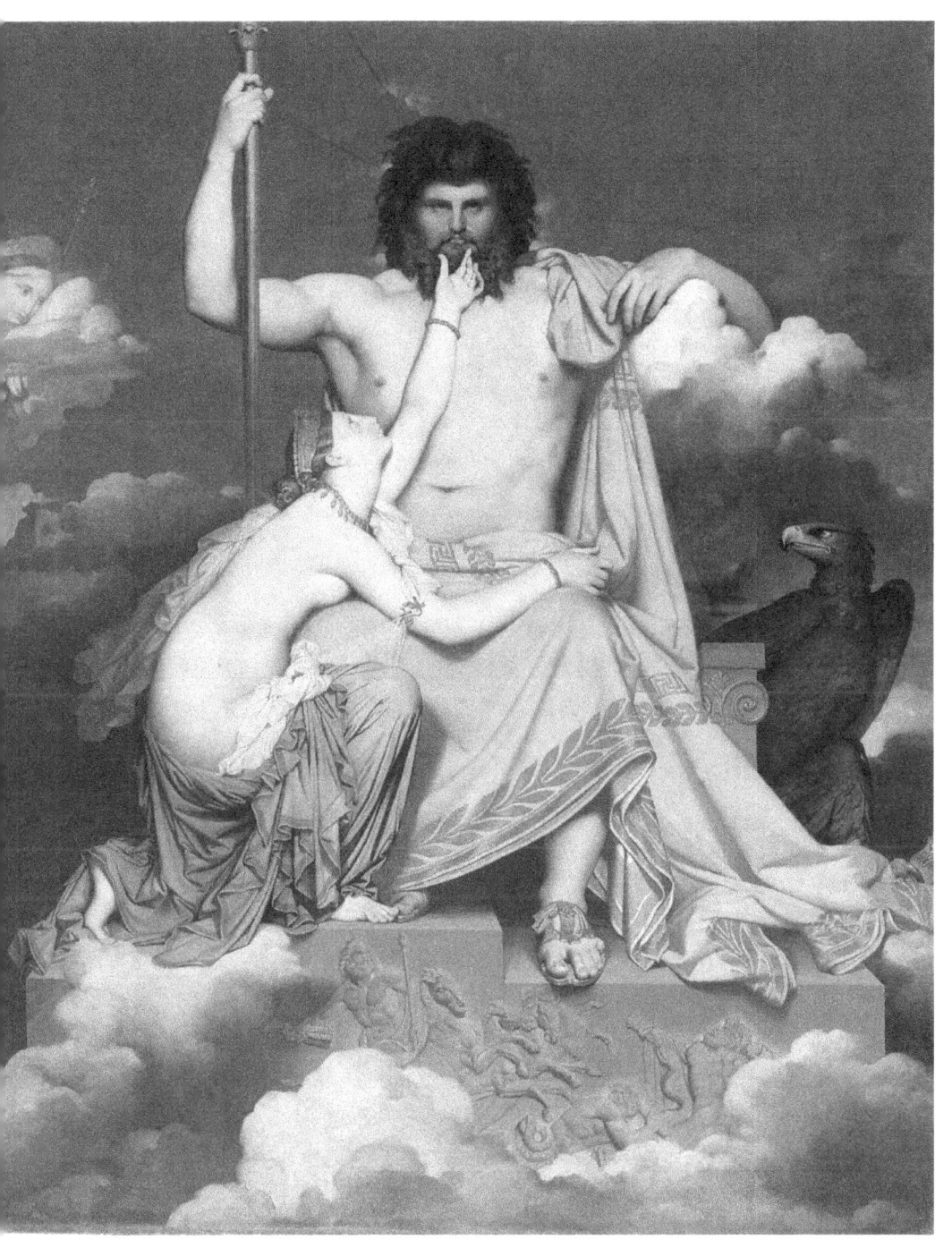

J.A.D. Ingres, Jupiter, 1811, Provence

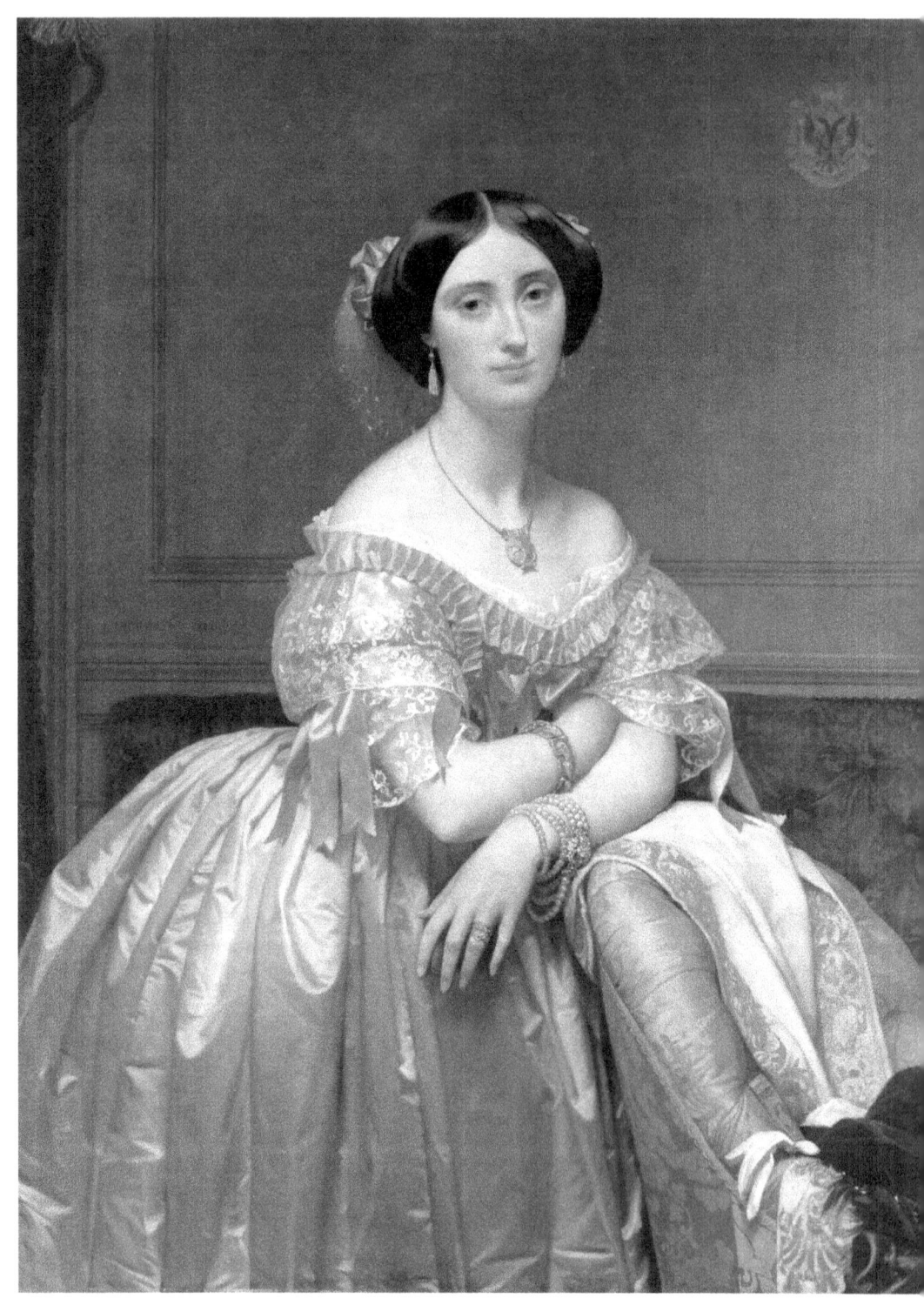

J.A.D.Ingres, Princesse Albert de Broglie, 1853, New York

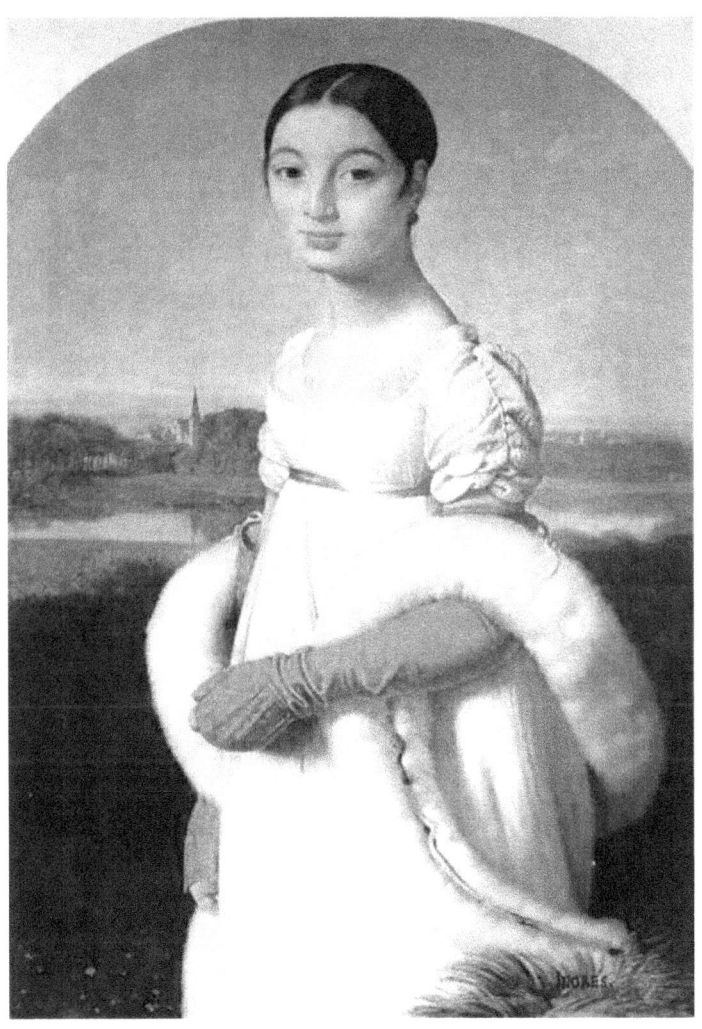

J.A.D. Ingres, Mademoiselle Riviere, 1805, Louvre

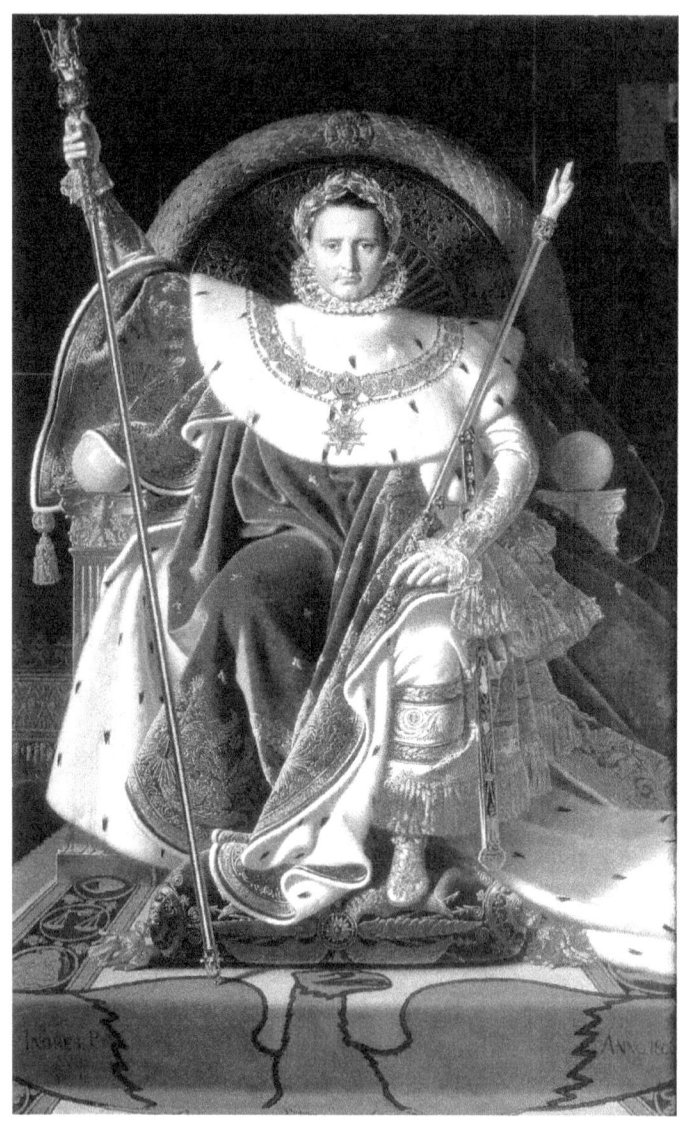

J.A.D. Ingres, Napoleon, 1806, Paris

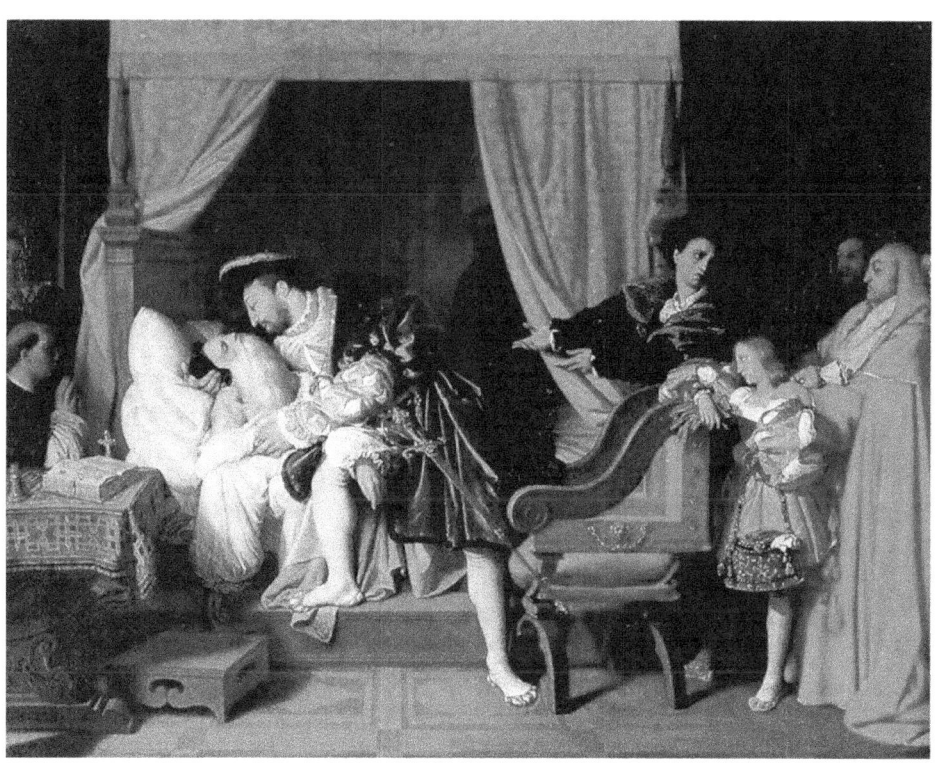

J.A.D. Ingres, The Death of Leonardo, 1818

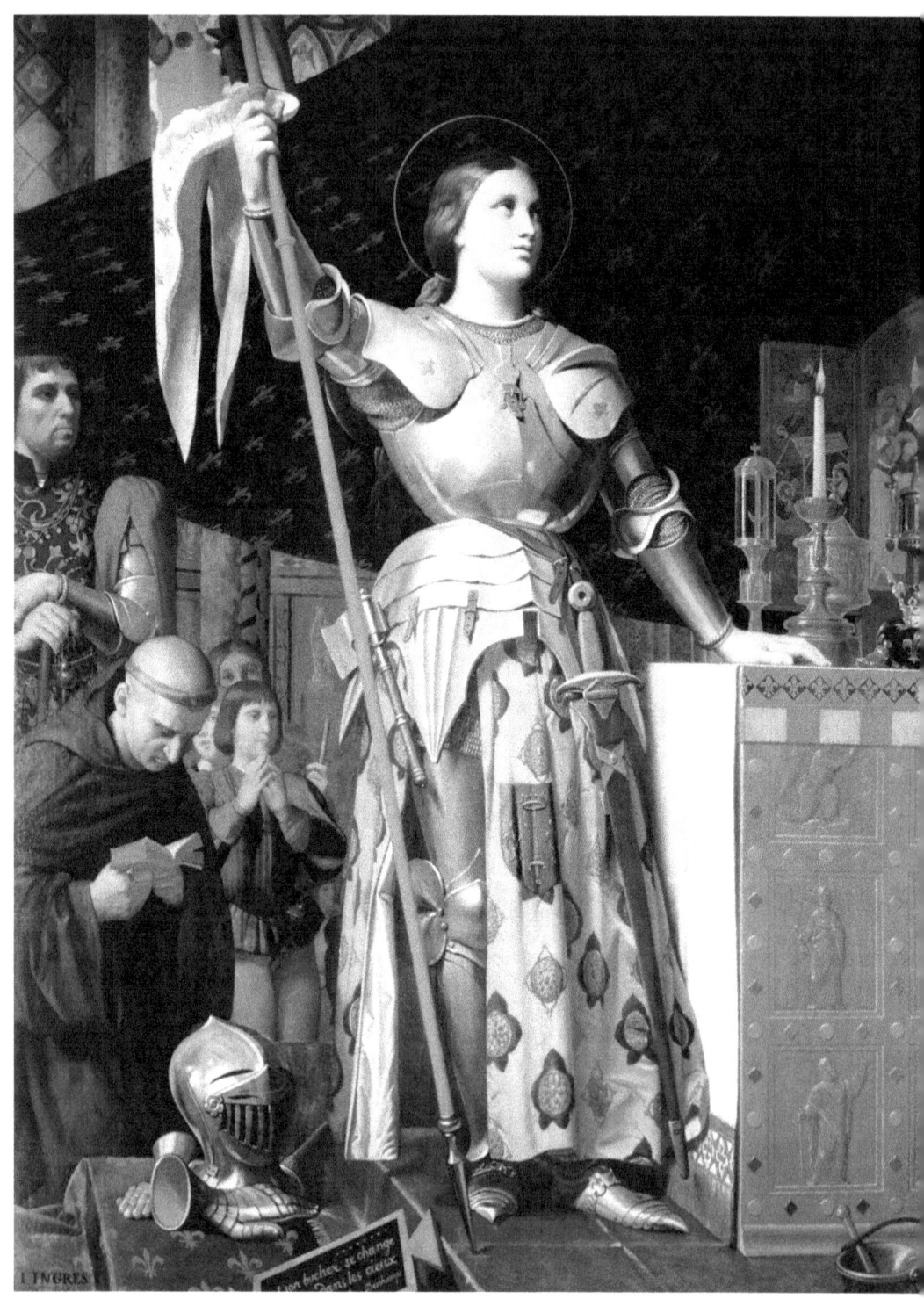

J.A.D. Ingres, The Coronation of Charles VII, Joan of Arc, 1854, Louvre

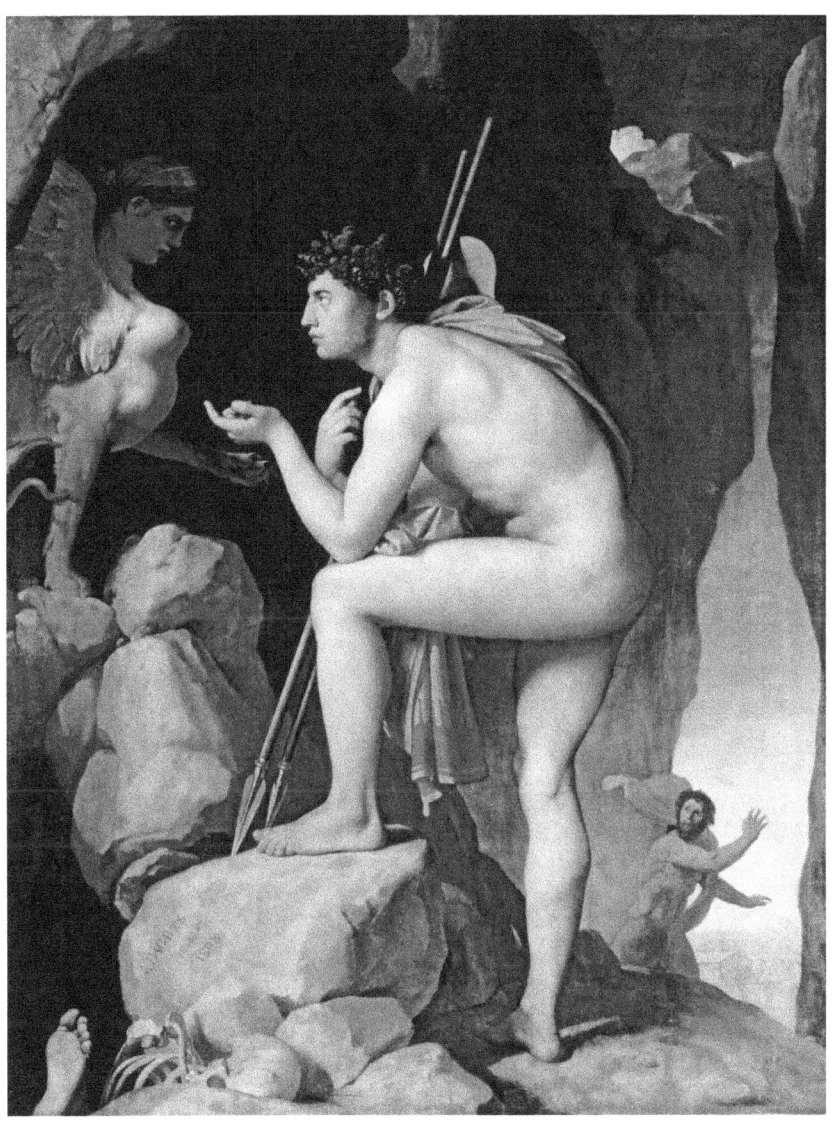

J.A.D.Ingres, Oedipus and the Sphinx, 1807, Louvre, Paris

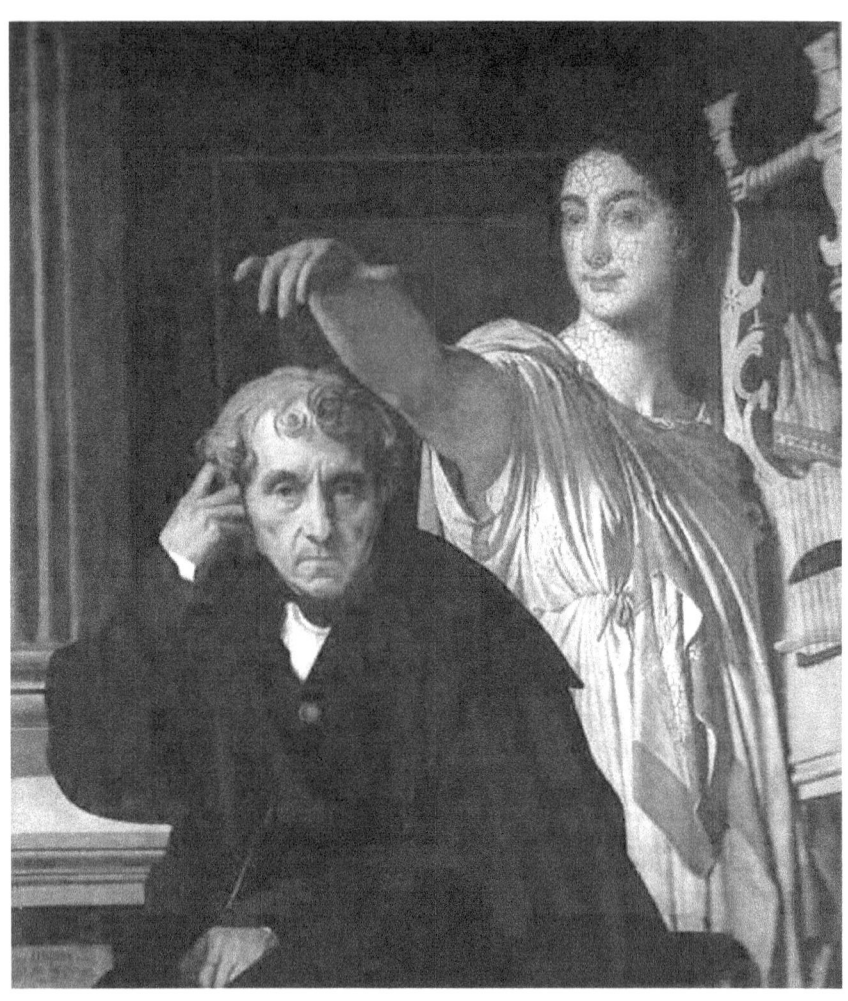

J.A.D. Ingres, Luigi Cherubini and the Muse of Lyric Poetry, 1842, Louvre

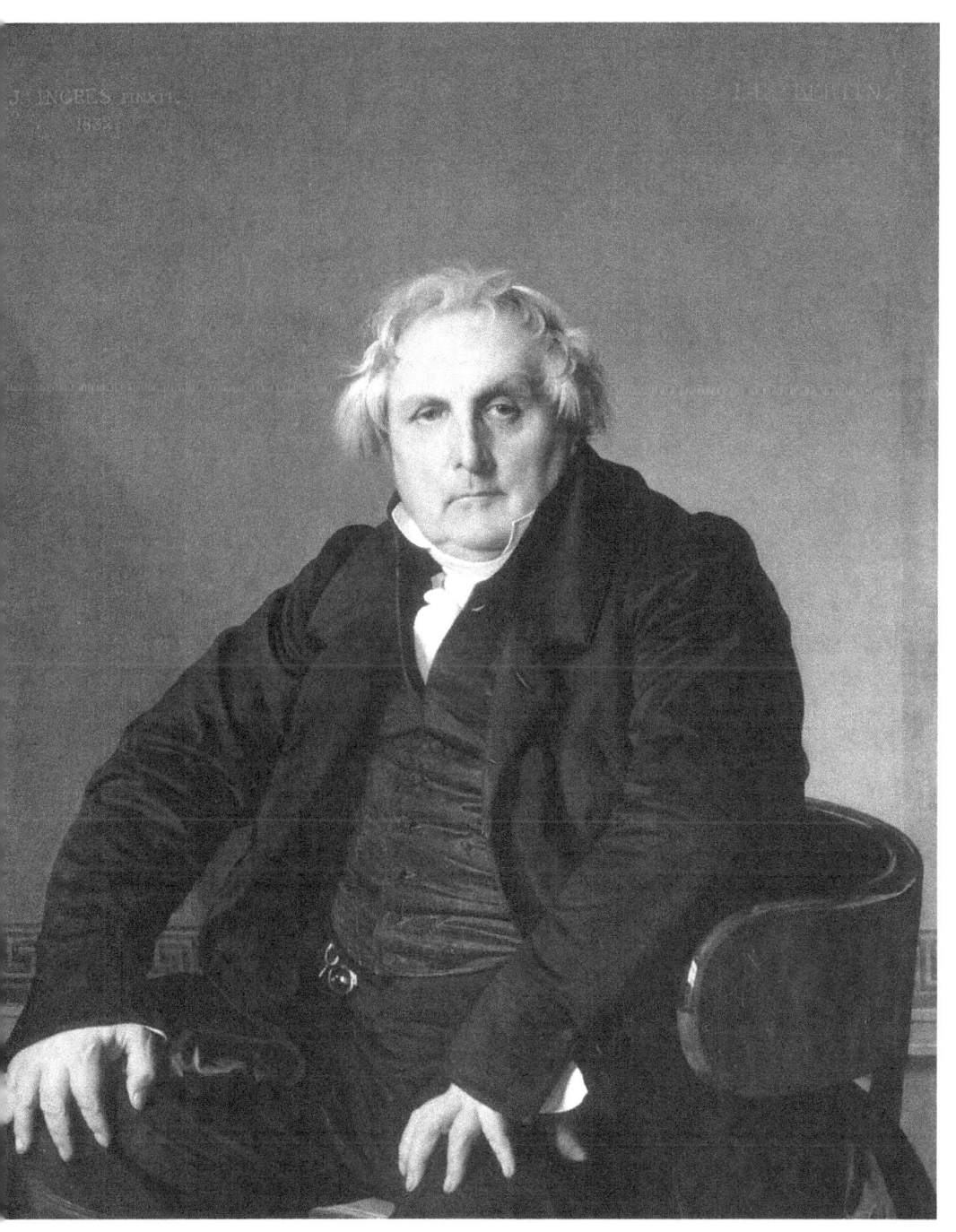

J.A.D. Ingres, Louis-Francois Bertin, 1832, Louvre

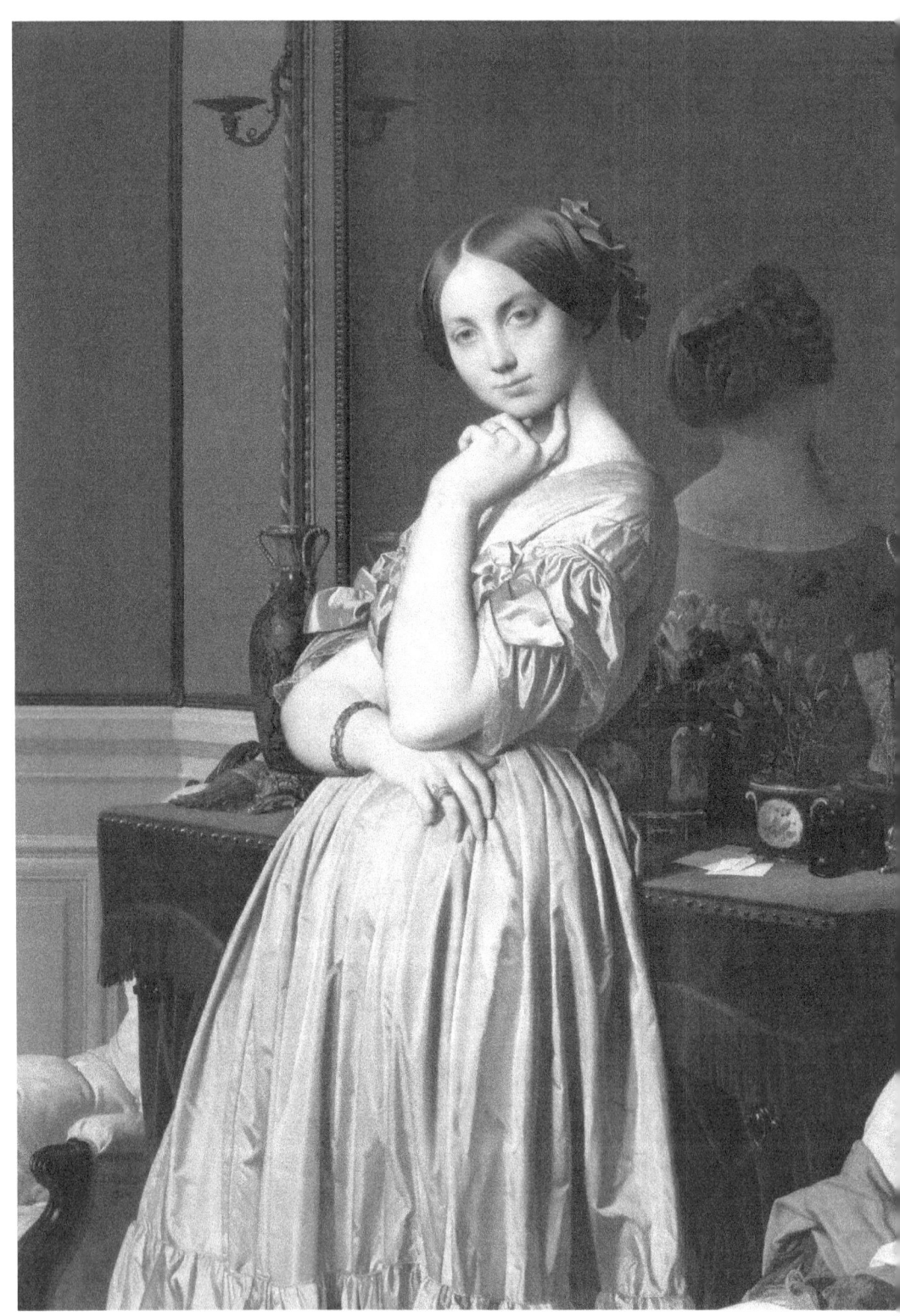

J.A.D. Ingres, Comtesse d'Haussonville, 1845, Frick Collection
(this page and over)

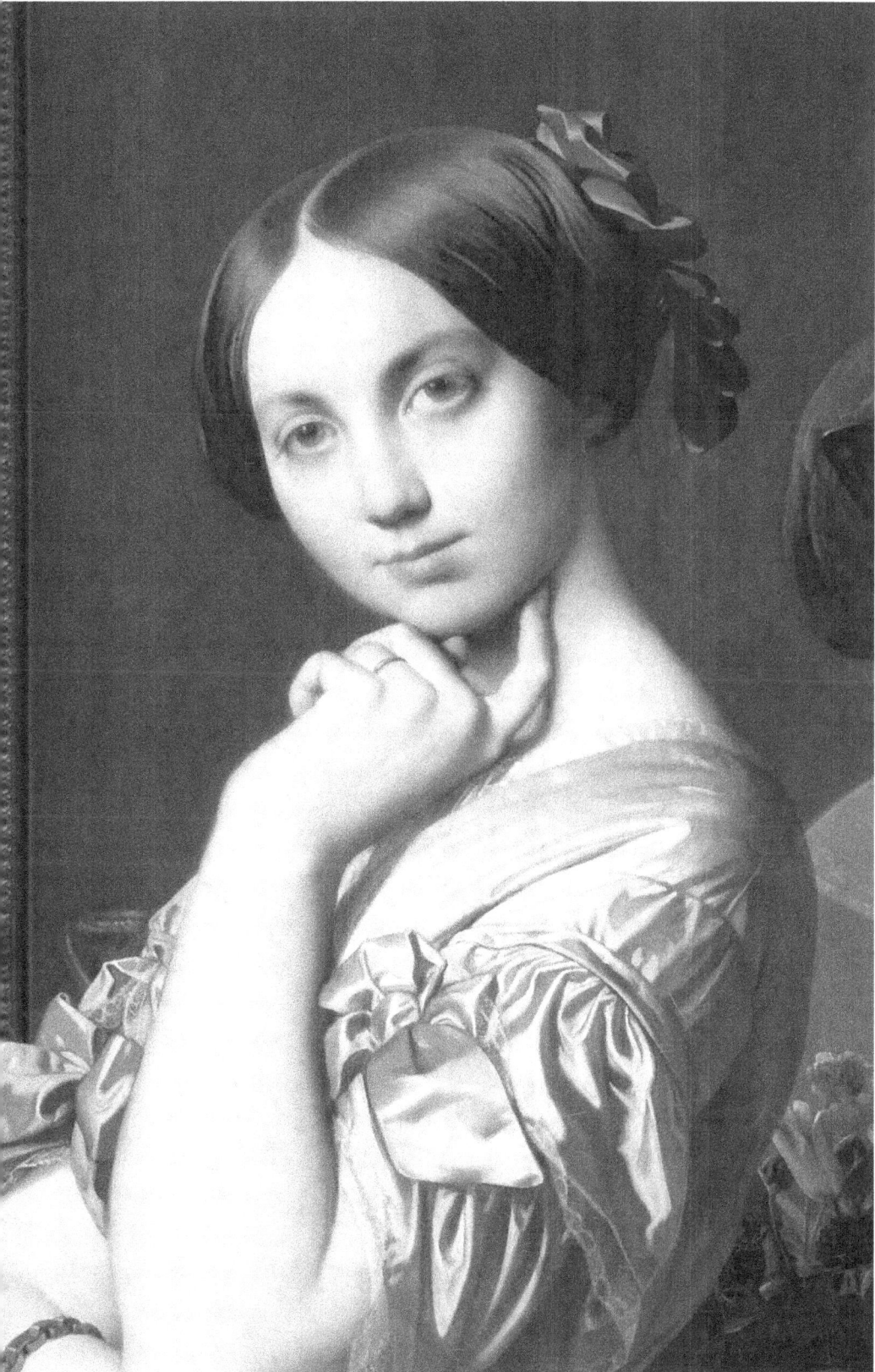

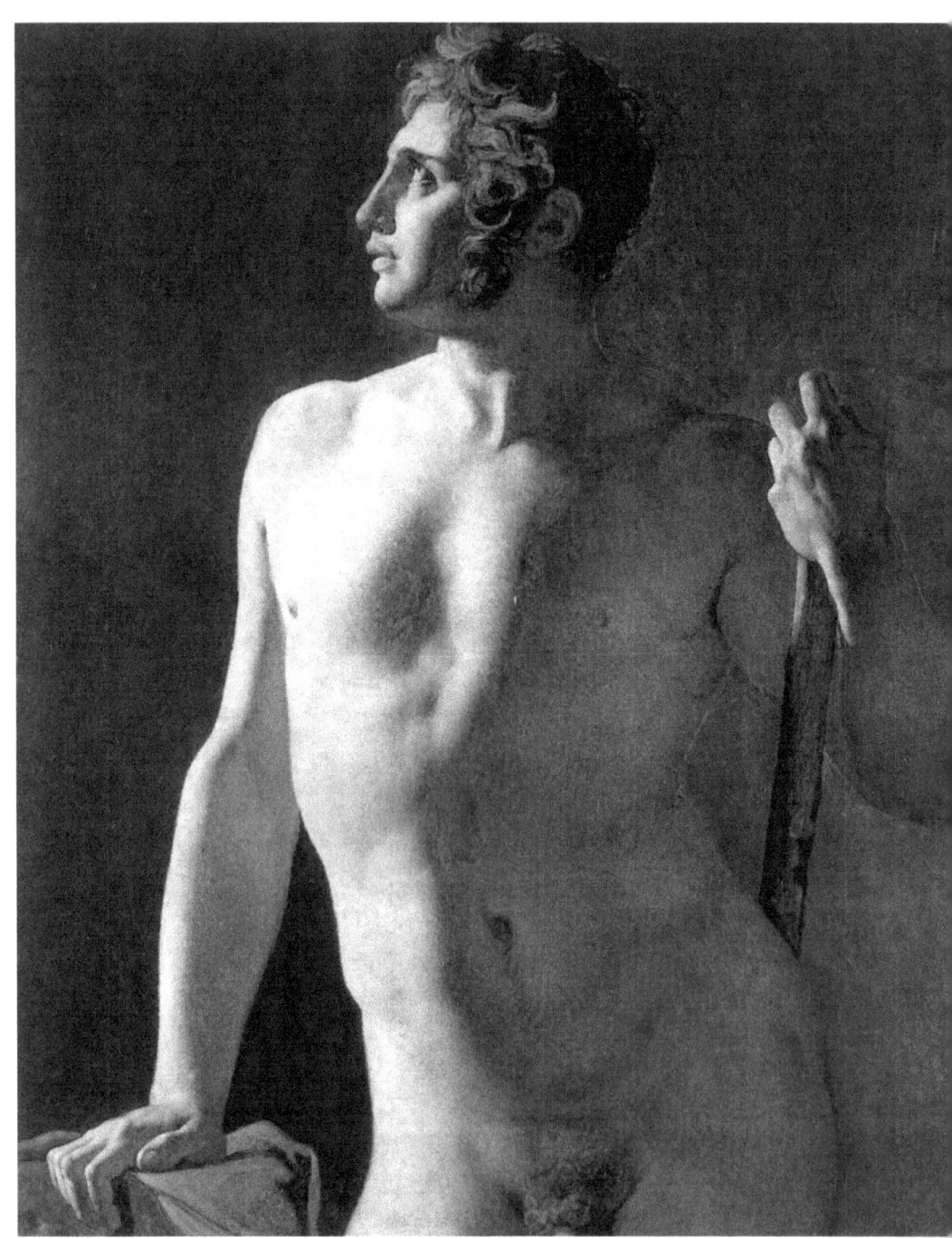

J.A.D. Ingres, Study of a Male Nude, 1801

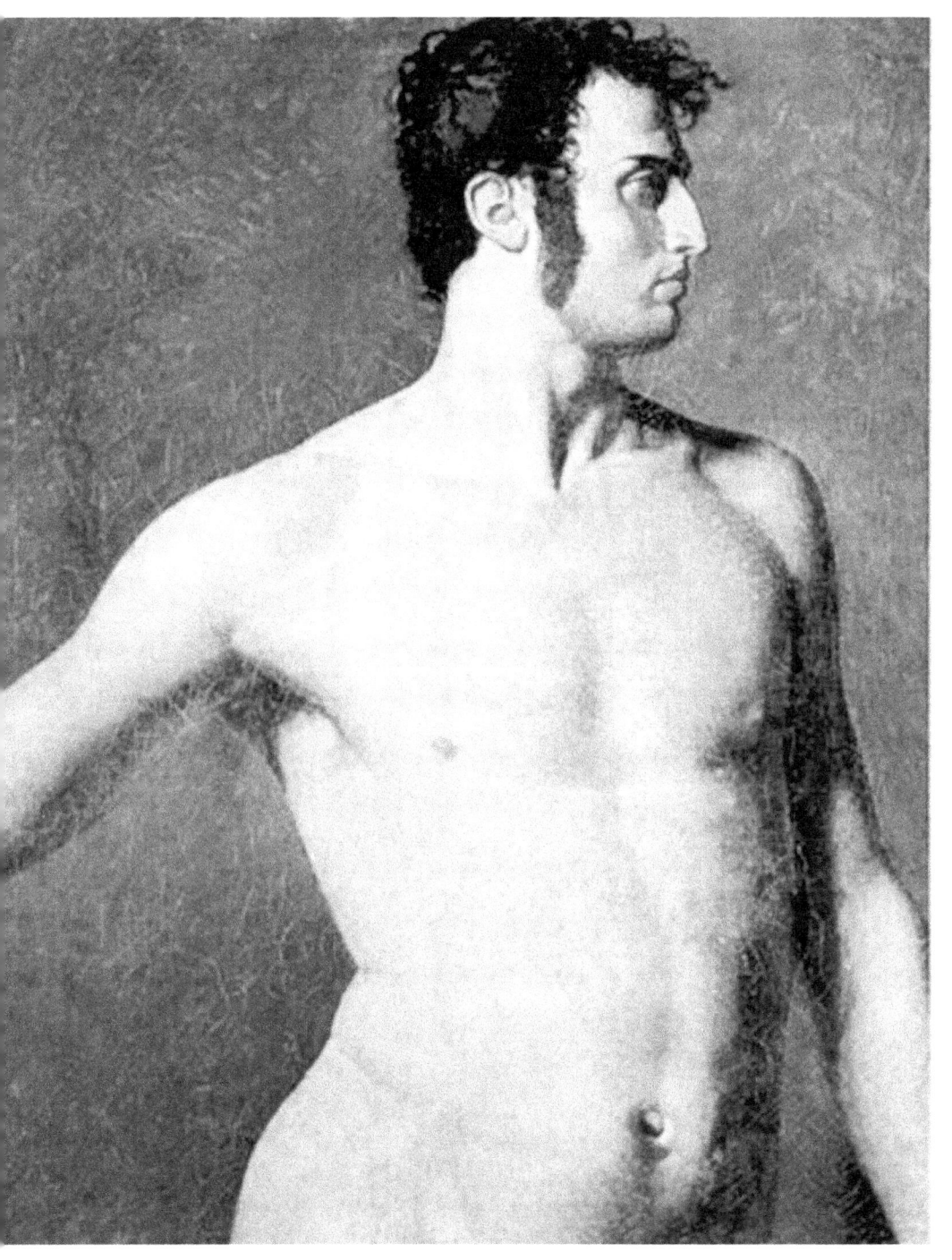

J.A.D. Ingres, Male Torso, 1801, Musée Ingres

On the following pages are some contemporaries of Ingres.

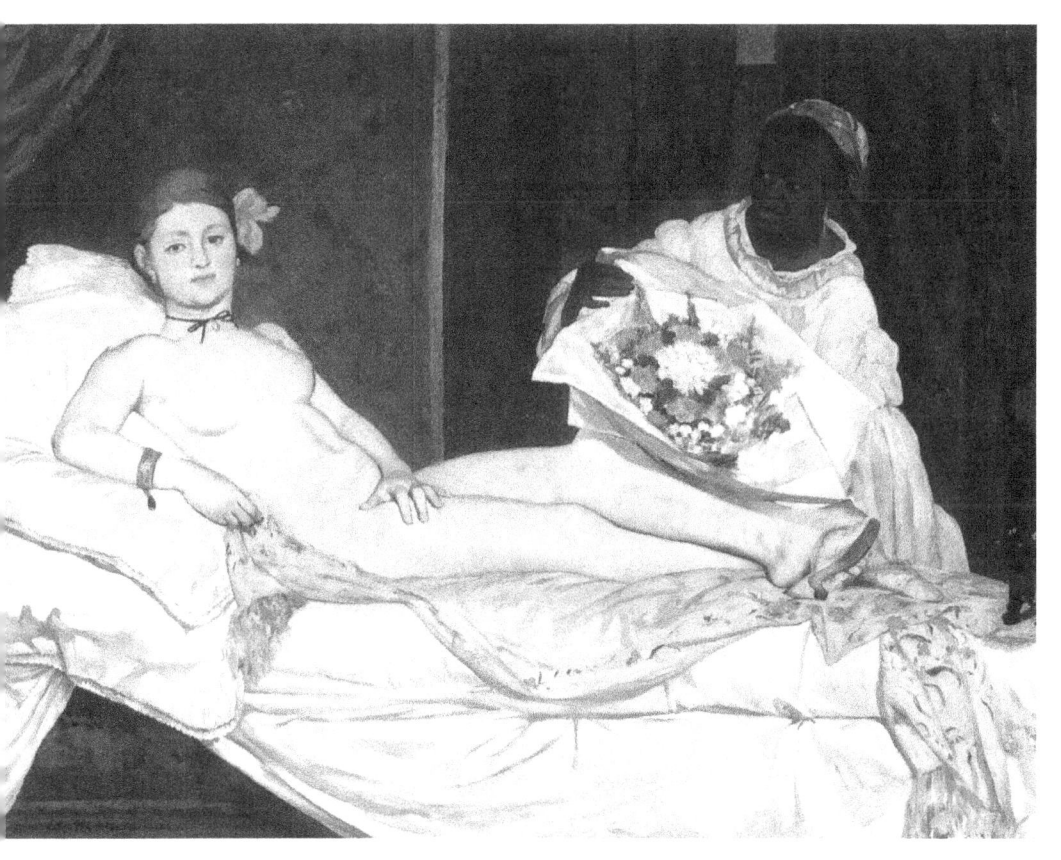

Edouard Manet, Olympia, Musée d'Orsay, Paris

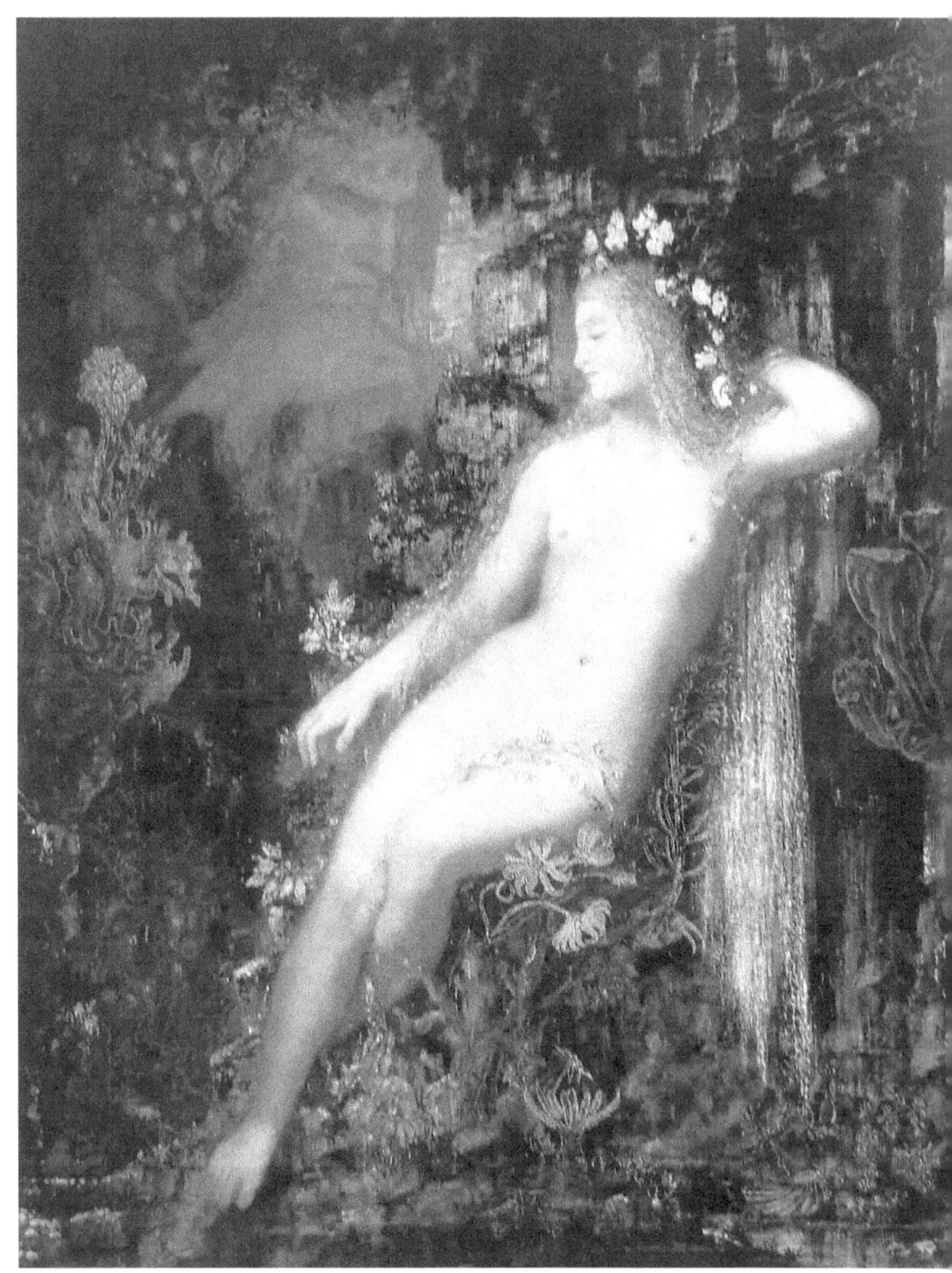

Gustave Moreau, Galatea, 1880

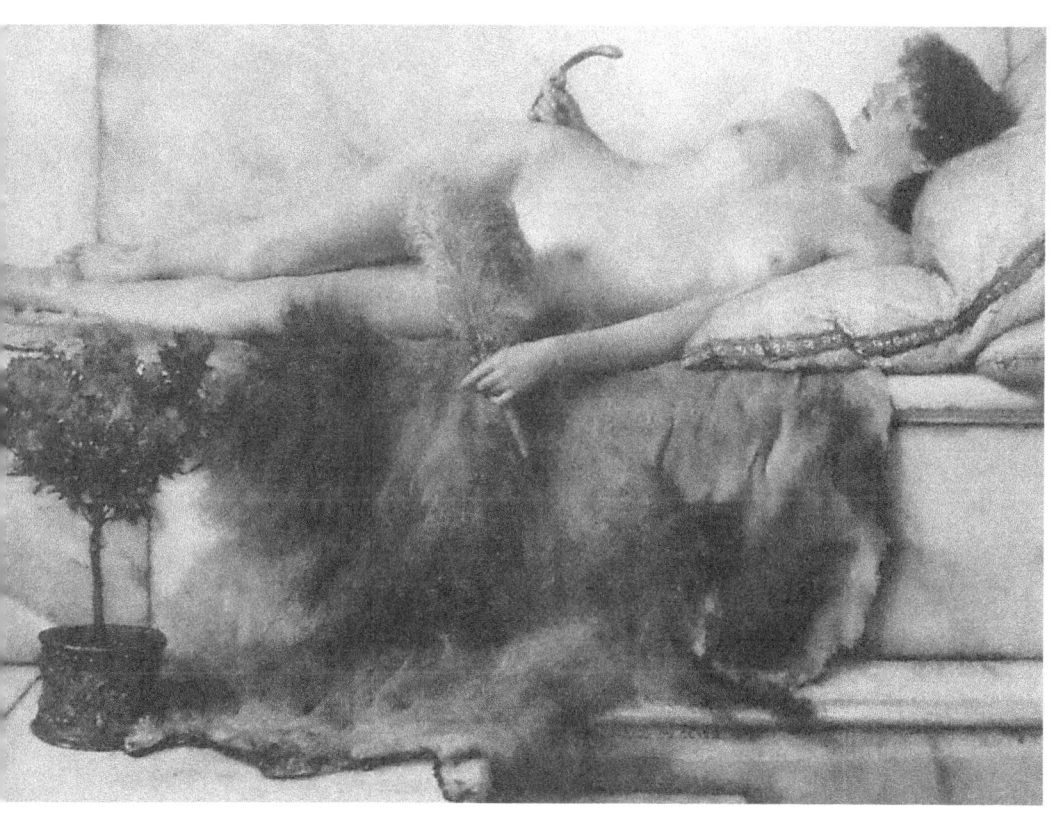

Lawrence Alma-Tadema, In the Tepidarium, 1881,
Lady Lever Art Gallery, Liverpool

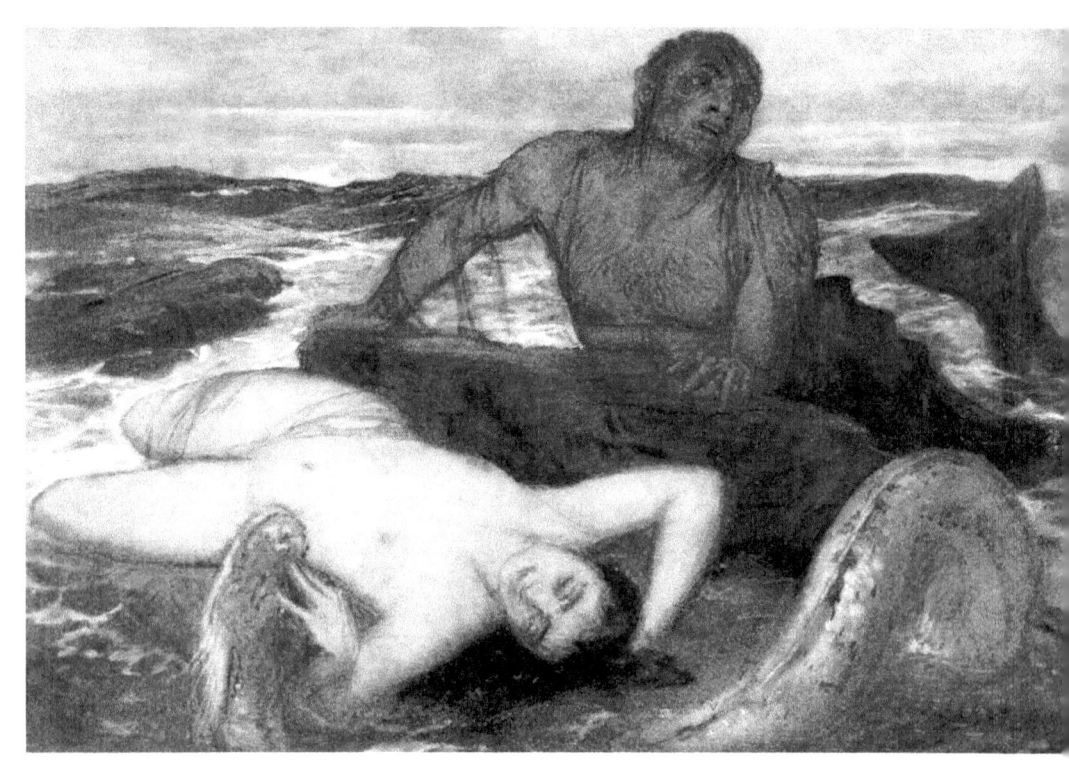

Arnold Böcklin, Triton and Nereid, 1877

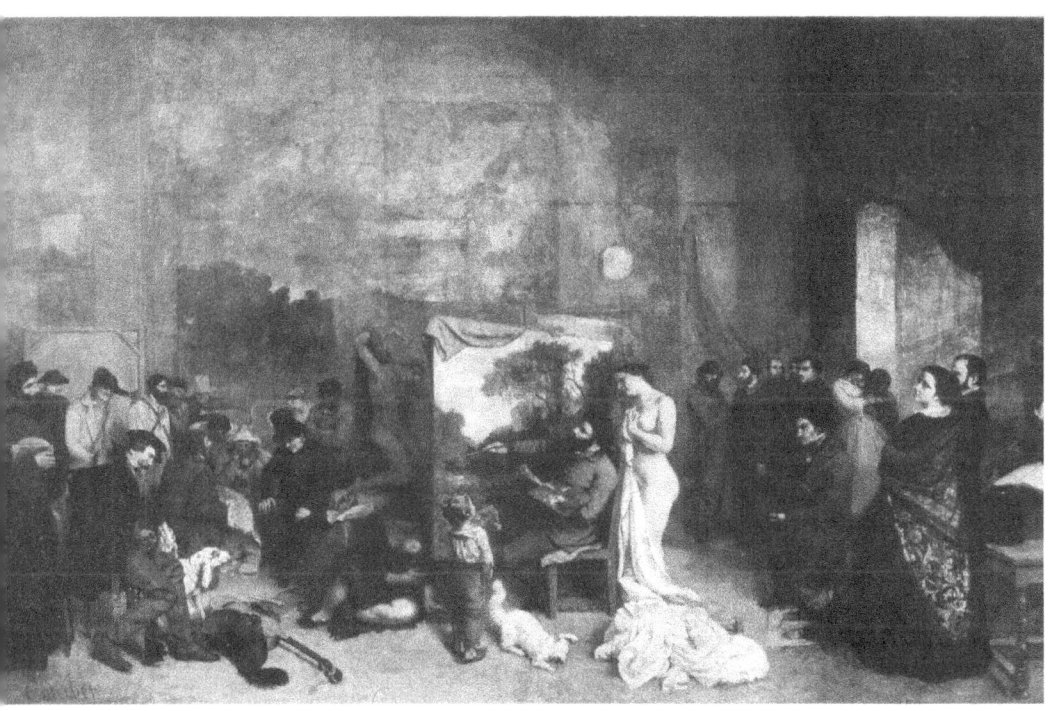

Gustave Courbet, The Studio, 1855, Musée d'Orsay, Paris

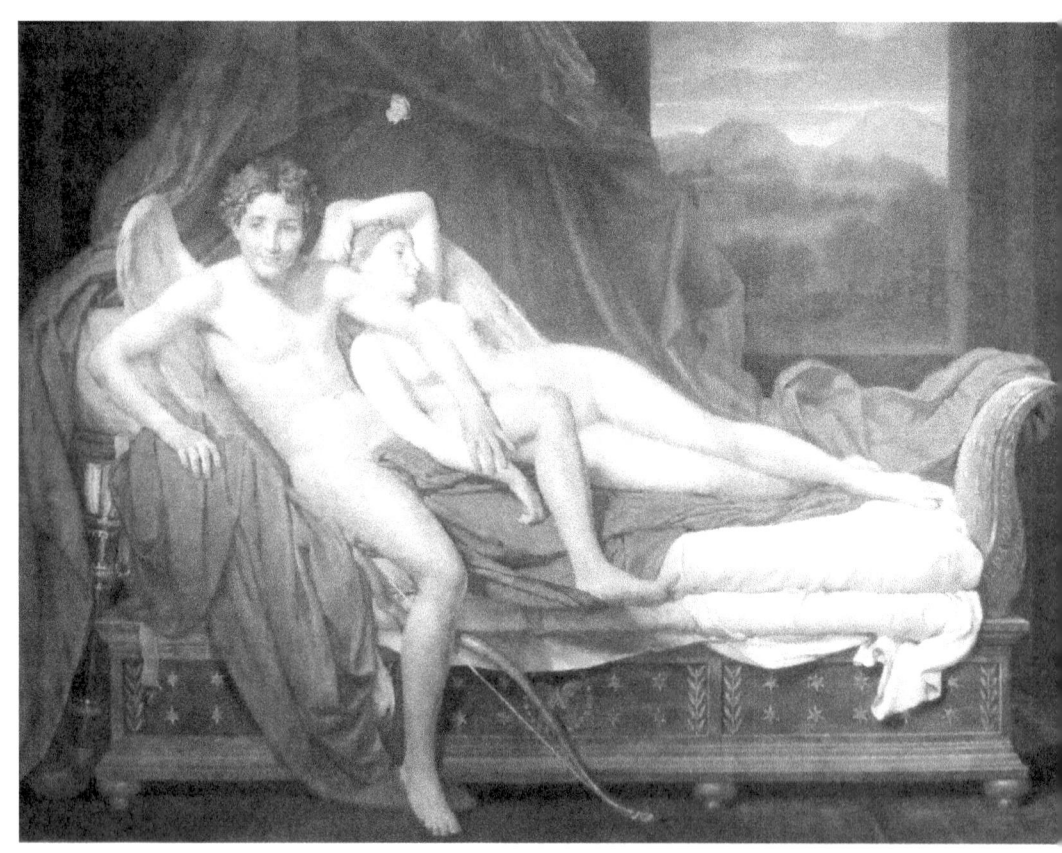

Jacques-Louis David, Cupid and Psyche, 1817,
Cleveland Museum of Art

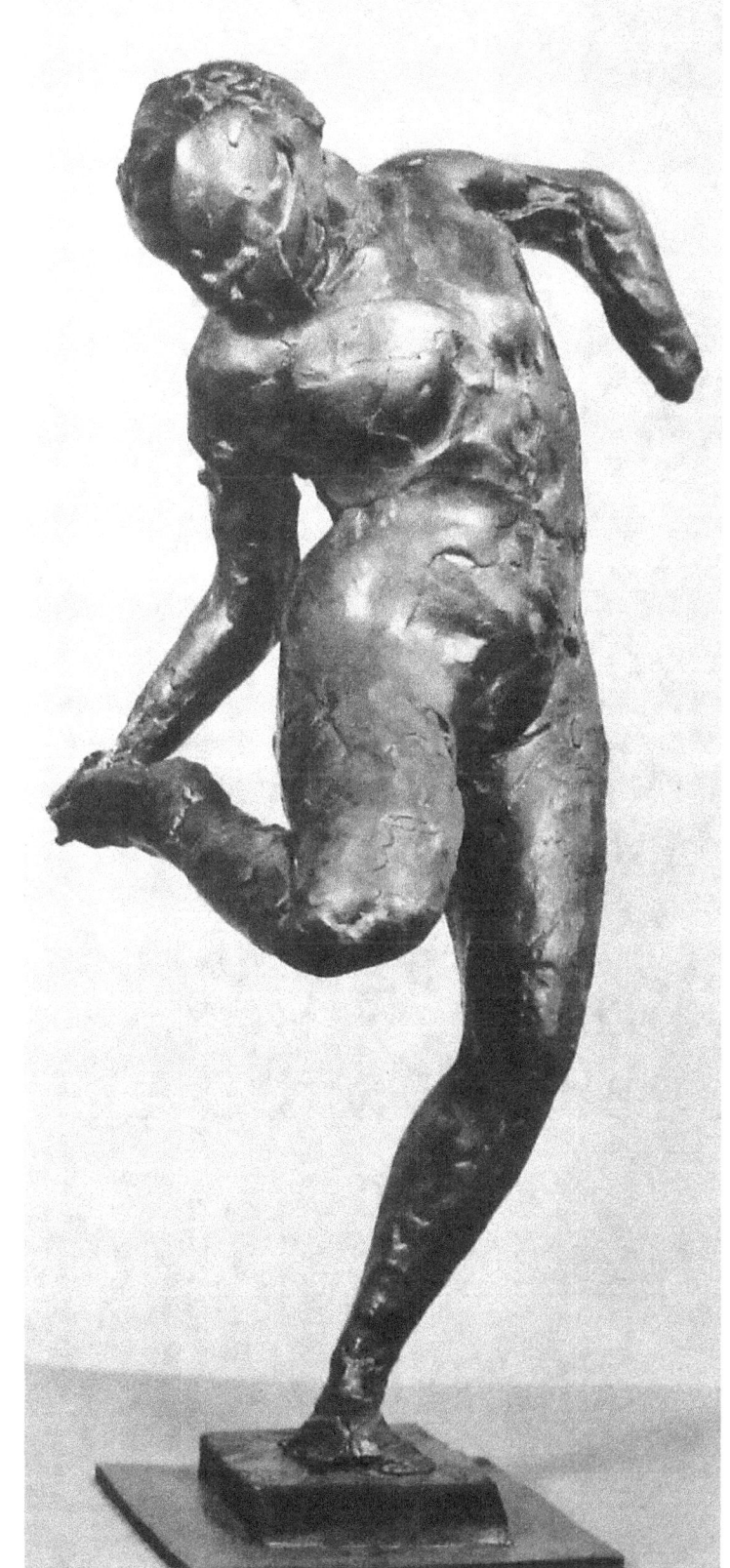

Edgar Degas,
Dancer Looking At
the Sole of Her
Right Foot, 1882-95,
New York

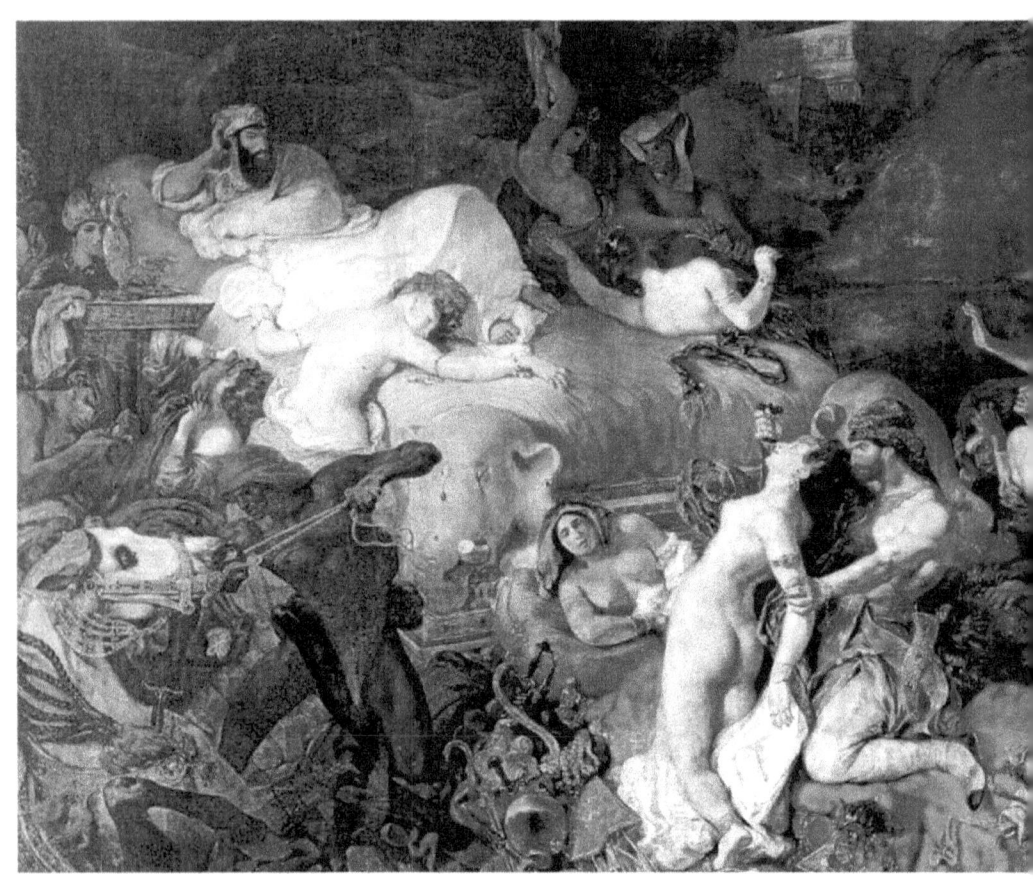

Eugène Delacroix, The Death of Sardanapalus, 1827
(this page and over).

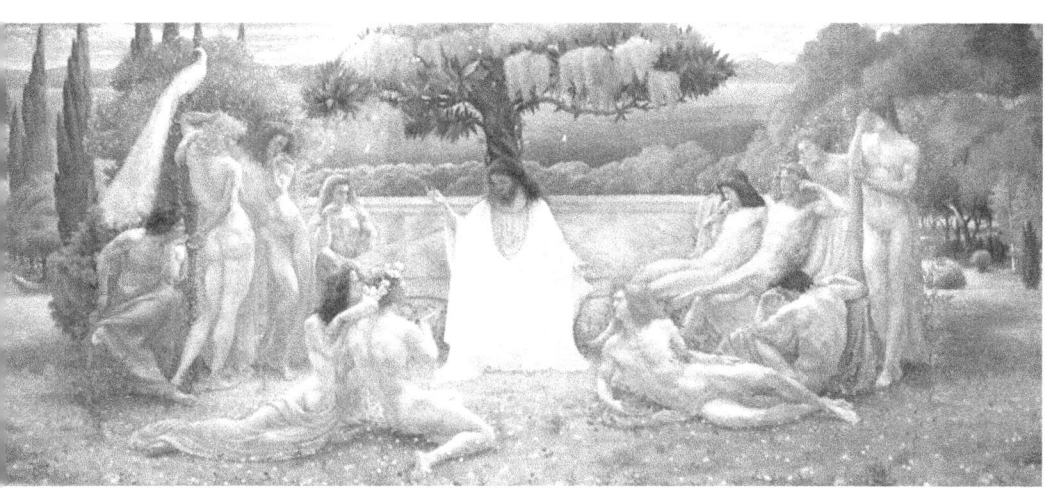

Jean Delville, The School of Plato, 1898

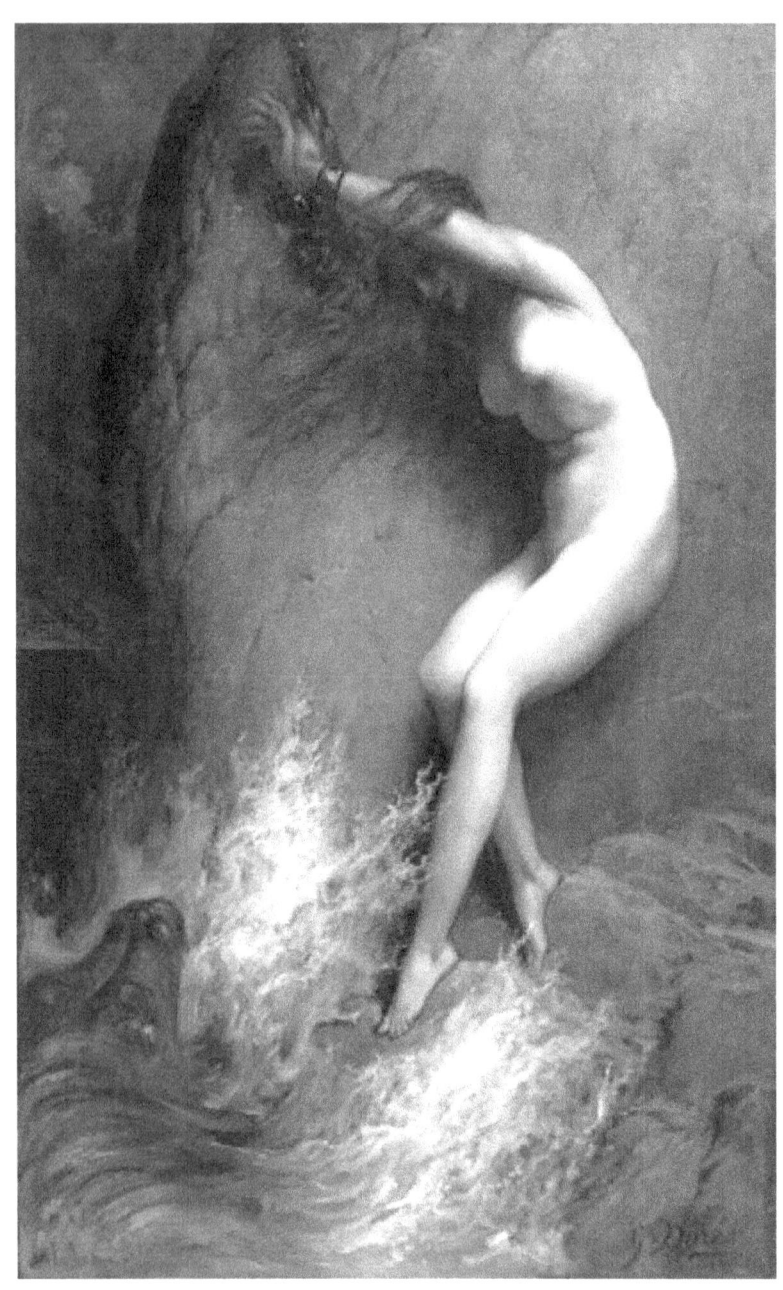

Gustave Doré

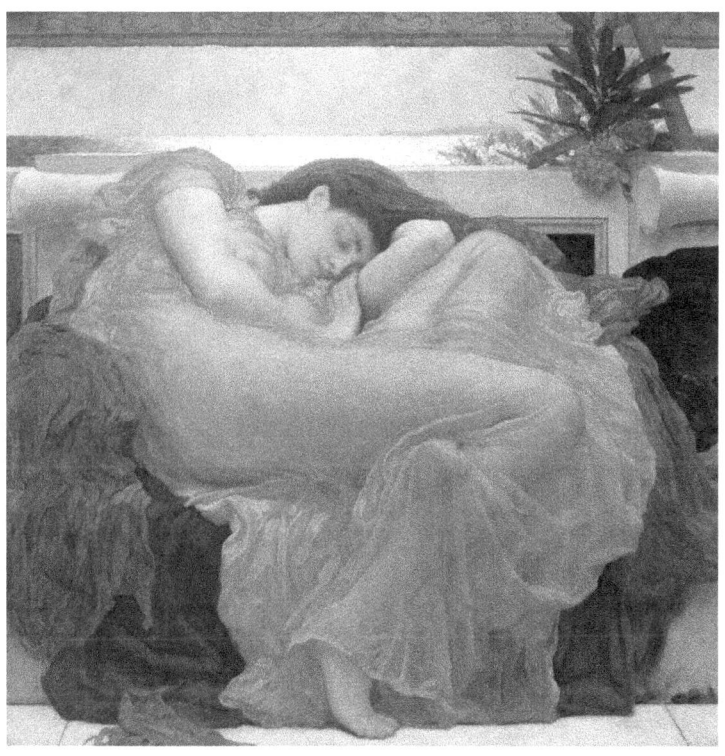

Lord Leighton, Flaming June, 1895, Puerto Rico

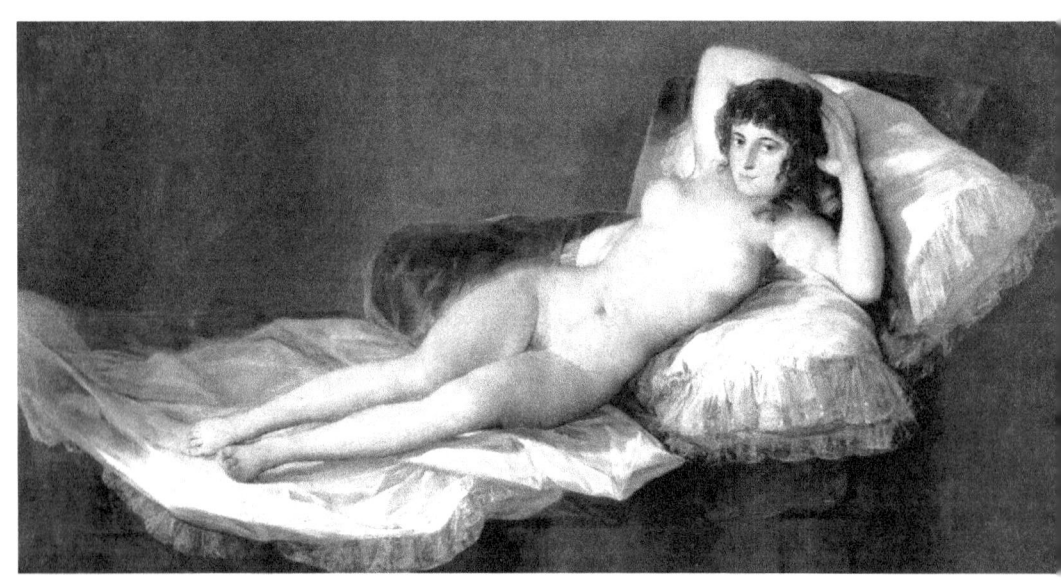

Francisco de Goya, Naked Maja, c. 1801, Prado, Madrid

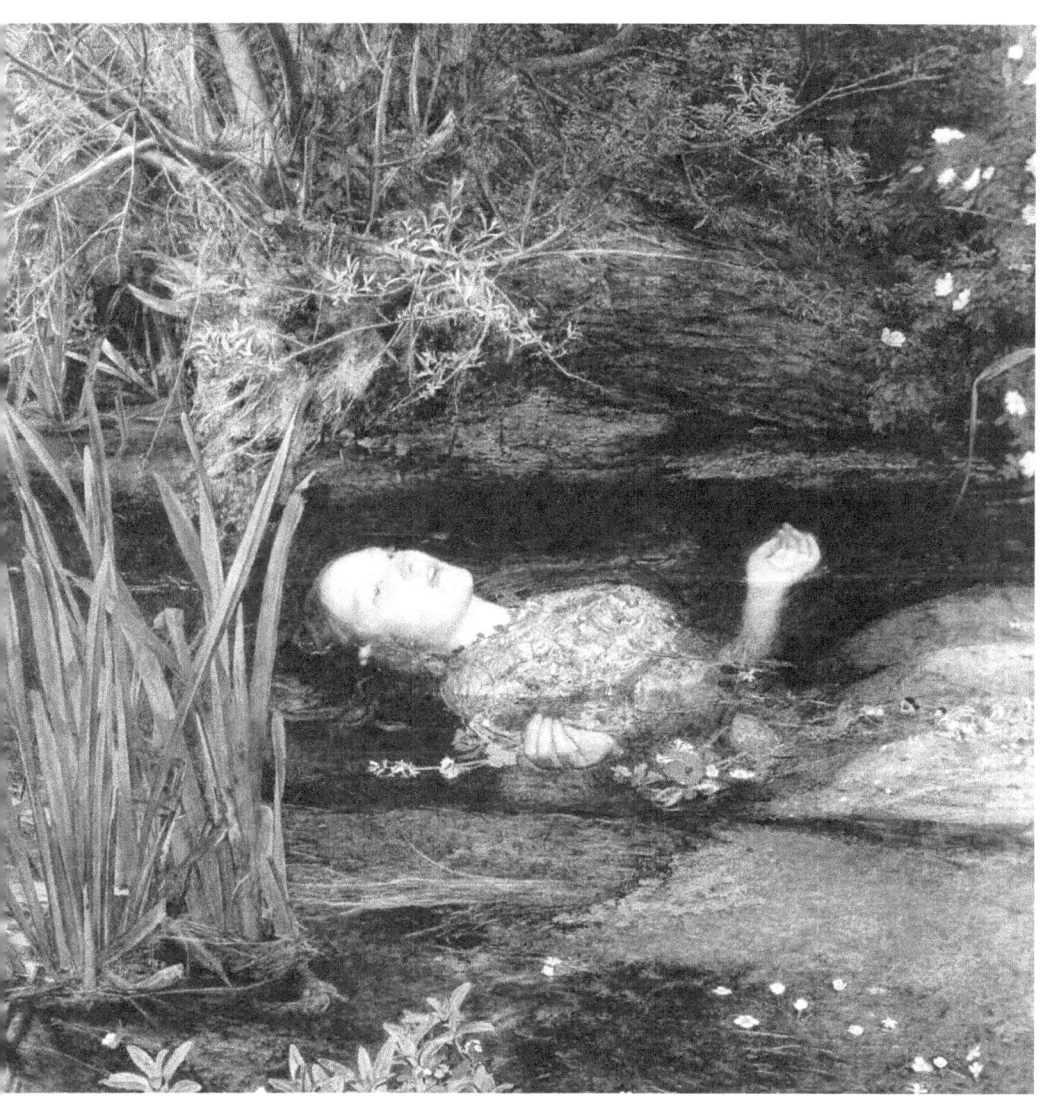

John Everett Millais, Ophelia.

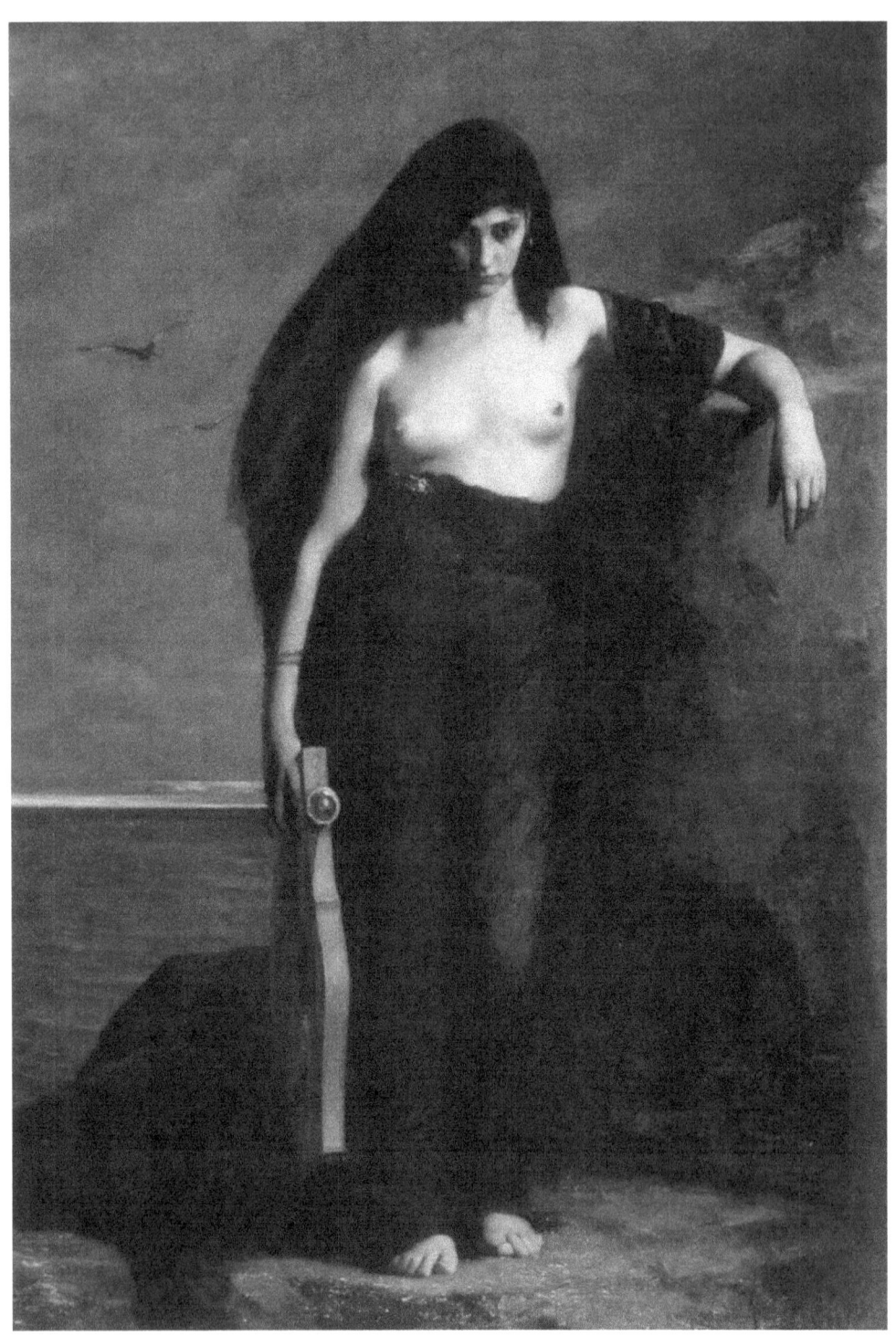

Charles Mengin, Sappho, 1867, Manchester

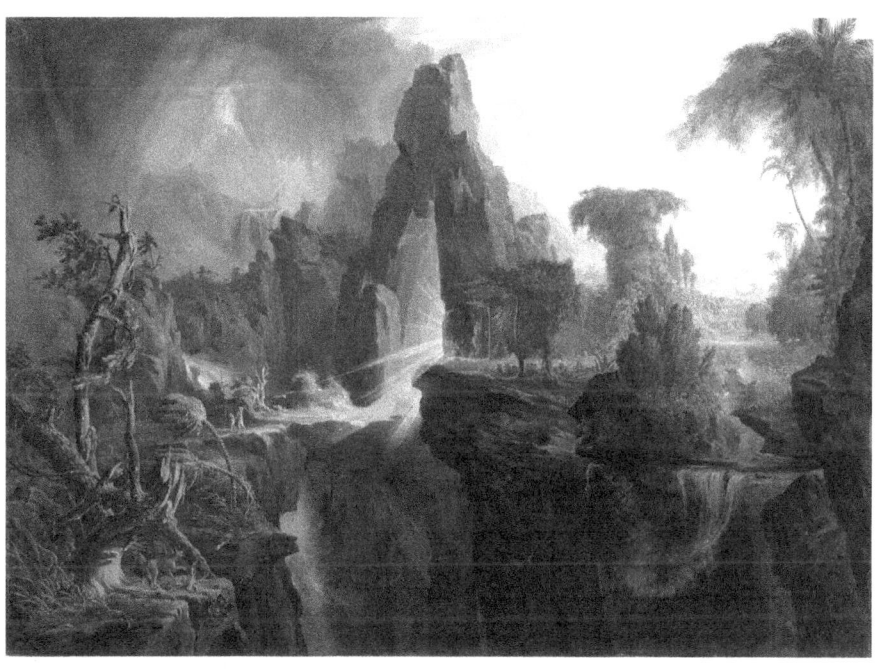

Thomas Cole, Expulsion From the Garden of Eden, 1828,
Museum of Fine Arts, Boston

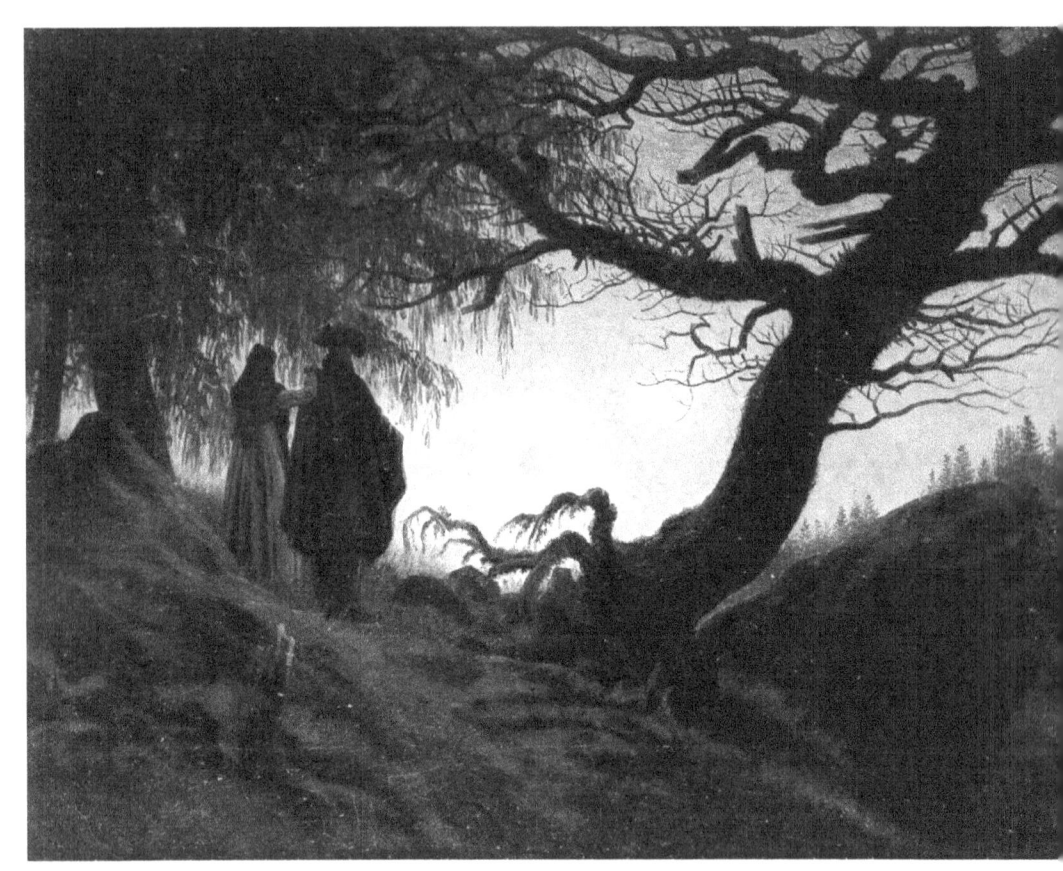

Caspar David Friedrich, Man and
Woman Contemplating the Moon,
1830-35, Alte Nationalgalerie

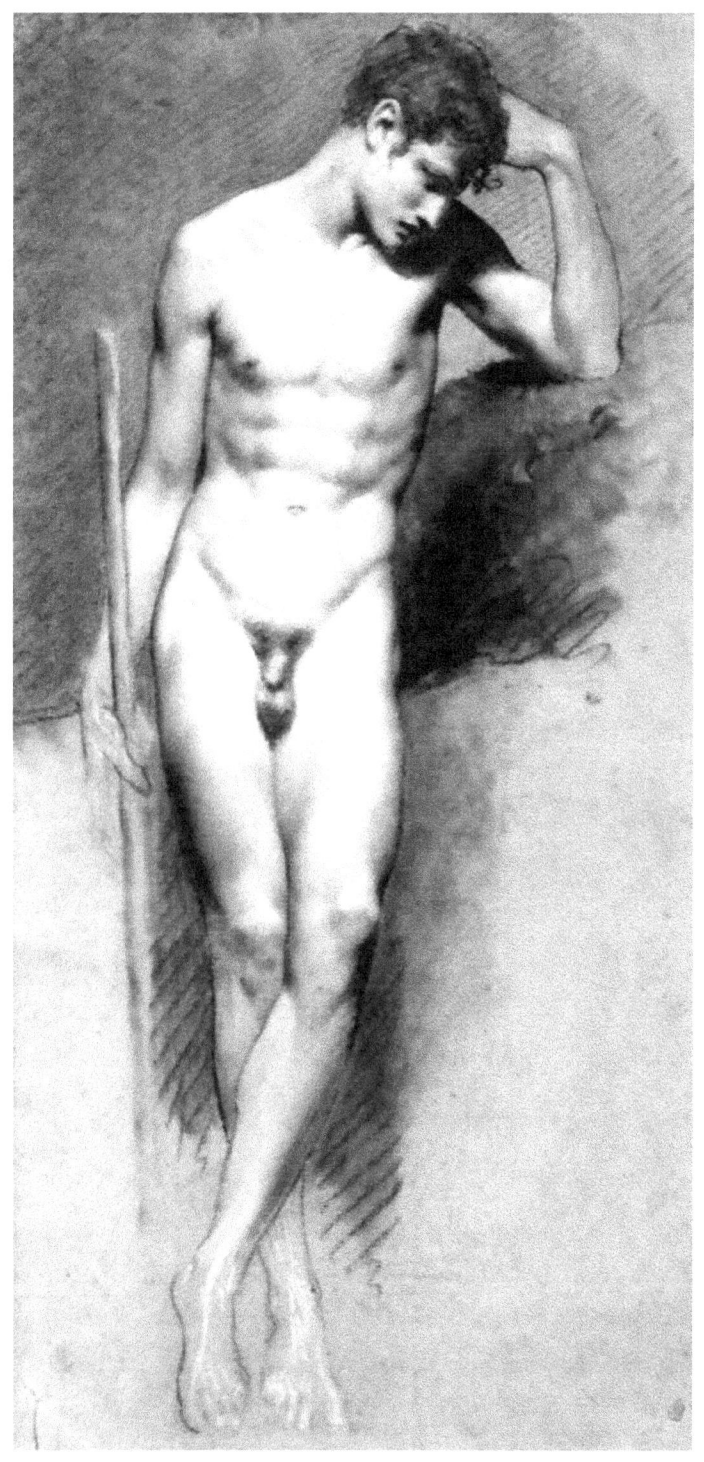

Pierre-Paul Prud'hon (1758-1823), Male Nude Standing

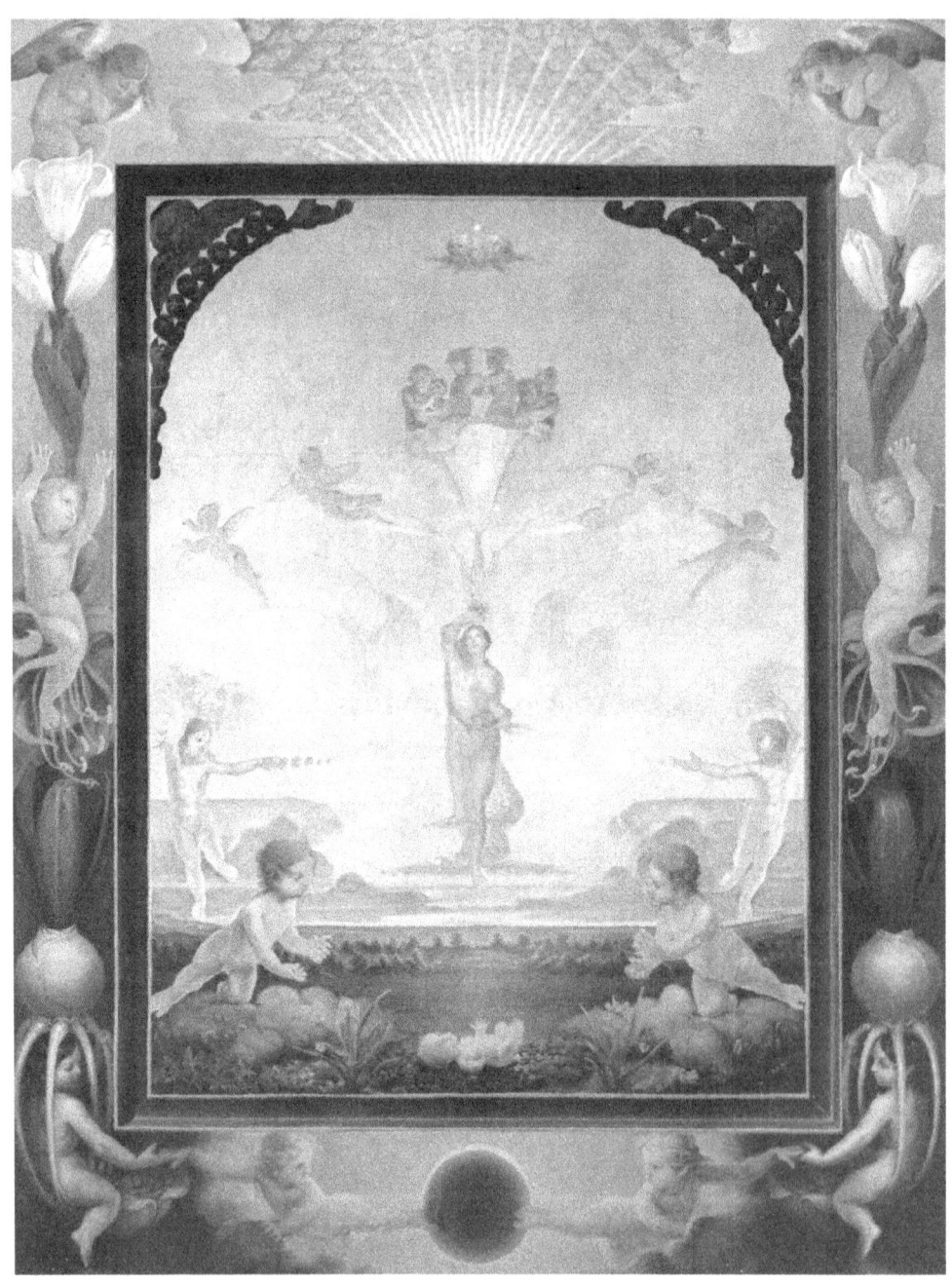

Philipp Otto Runge, Morning, 1808, Hamburg

J.M.W. Turner, The Blue Rigi, Lake of Lucerne, Sunrise,
1842, Clore Gallery, London

NOTES ON WORKS

LA VIERGE À L'HOSTIE
(In the Louvre)

This picture of "La Vierge à l'Hostie" is a repetition, with variations, of another painted by Ingres in 1840 for the Czar Nicholas, in which he had represented on either side of the Virgin the two patron saints of Russia, St. Nicholas and St. Alexander. In the Louvre picture, which is signed "J. Ingres, 1854," the two saints have been replaced by two angels. Probably in no other picture from his hand is the artist's passionate admiration for Raphael so clearly displayed.

MADAME RIVIÈRE
(In the Louvre)

This portrait of "Madame Rivière" is one of the most characteristic works of Ingres' first period – the period (1800-1806) of that six years' weary wait to depart for Rome which the bankruptcy of the public exchequer compelled the young artist to submit to. In a list of his works executed immediately before his first portrait of "Bartolini," painted in 1805, Ingres mentions the portraits of "M. Rivière, Madame Rivière, and their ravishing daughter." This fixes the date of these three portraits as about 1804. These are often spoken of by French critics as typical specimens of the artist's "Pre-Raphaelite manner." All three portraits are now in the Louvre.

L'APOTHEOSE D'HOMERE
(In the Louvre)

This large and famous picture was commissioned to fill the ceiling of one of the galleries of the Louvre. It is signed "Ingres pingbat, anno 1827." It cost the master more research and trouble than any of his other works. This is proved by the number of painted studies, some of them superior to the finished picture itself, and the repeated references to it in his letters and note-books. Homer is being crowned by Victory, and the two beautiful female figures seated at his feet represent the *Iliad* and the *Odyssey*. Around Homer are the painters, sculptors, and musicians whom the artist wished to glorify. "To his great regret," he said he felt compelled to exclude Goethe, because he found too many "faults" in his writings. But Shakespeare and Pope were admitted. In his last version of this subject, made in 1865, Shakespeare was also finally expelled.

M. BERTIN
(In the Louvre)

This portrait represents the famous "Bertin ainé, the director of the *Journal des Débats*." It is signed "J. Ingres, pinxit 1832," and was exhibited at the Salon of 1833.

CHÉRUBINI
(In the Louvre)

This "portrait picture" was begun in Rome in 1839, but was only finished in Paris in 1842. The painter's first intention was to represent only the figure of Chérubini, but afterwards he had the canvas enlarged to make room behind the musician for the figure of the "Muse of lyrical poetry, mother of the sacred hymns." It is doubtful whether this addition is an improvement.

LE DUC D'ORLÉANS
(Musée de Versailles)

This grave and dignified portrait of the Duke of Orleans was ordered by the King in 1842. It is remarkable for the minuteness and care with which all the details of the uniform and the accessories are rendered.

JEANNE D'ARC
(In the Louvre)

The picture of "Joan of Arc assisting at the Consecration of Charles VII. in the Cathedral of Reims" was painted for the gallery of Versailles, but is now in the Louvre. It is signed "J. Ingres, 1854." The figure, the maid's squire, standing immediately behind the kneeling priest, is said to be a portrait of the artist himself.

BIBLIOGRAPHY

The authoritative French accounts of Ingres' life and work (from which the foregoing sketch has been compiled) are:–

Comte Henri Delaborde. – Ingres, sa vie, ses travaux, sa doctrine (1870).

Charles Blanc. – Ingres (1870).

Henry Lapauze. – L'Œuvre de Ingres (in "Melanges sur l'Art Français," 1905).

Jules Momméja. – Ingres ("Les Grands Artistes" series).

T. de Wyzewa. – L'Œuvre peint de Jean-Dominique Ingres (1907).

Boyer d'Agen. – Ingres d'apres une Correspondence inédite (1909).

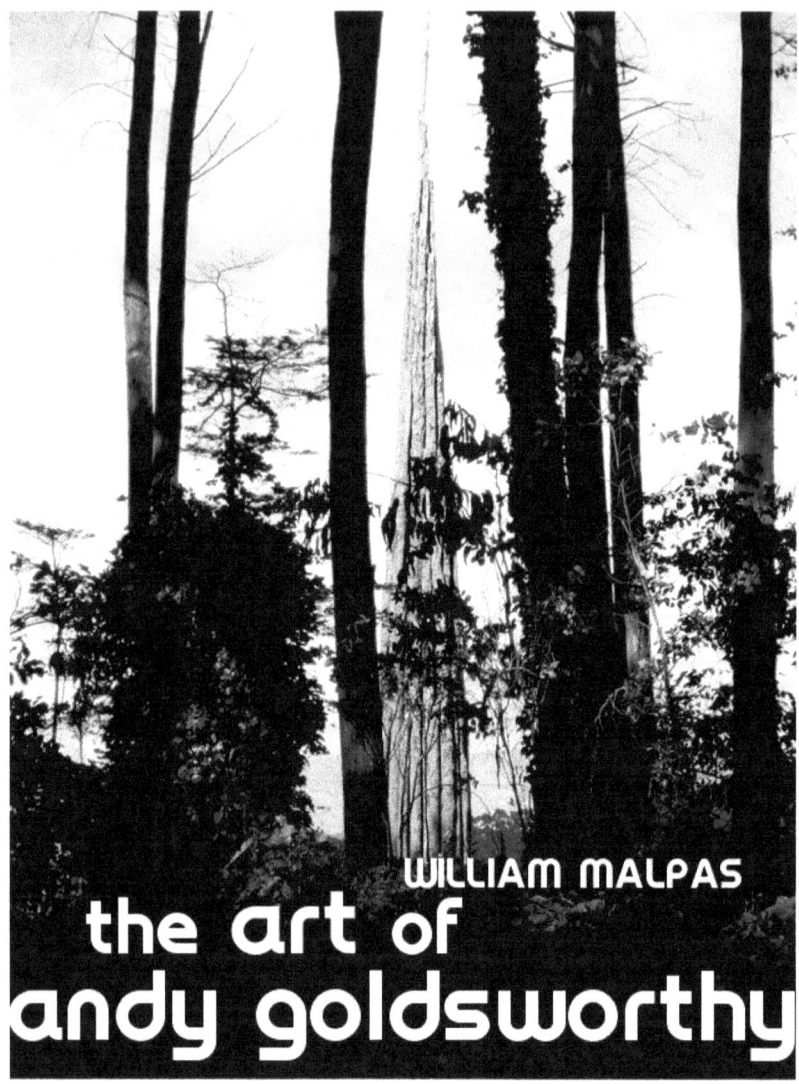

WILLIAM MALPAS
the art of
andy goldsworthy

This is the most comprehensive and detailed account of the art of Andy Goldsworthy available.

    This study of Andy Goldsworthy discusses all of Goldsworthy's major exhibitions, books and projects, including the *Sheepfolds* project; *Garden of Stones* in New York; TV and dance collaborations; and the books *Wood, Stone, Time* and *Passage*. William Malpas surveys all of Goldsworthy's output, and analyzes his relation with other land artists such as Robert Smithson, the Christos, Walter de Maria, Chris Drury, Richard Long and David Nash; women sculptors; sculpture in the modern era; and Goldsworthy's place in the contemporary British art scene.

The book has been updated and revised for this new edition.

ISBN 9781861714107 Pbk   ISBN 9781861714114 Hbk
Fully illustrated   www.crmoon.com

MAURICE SENDAK

& the art of children's book illustration

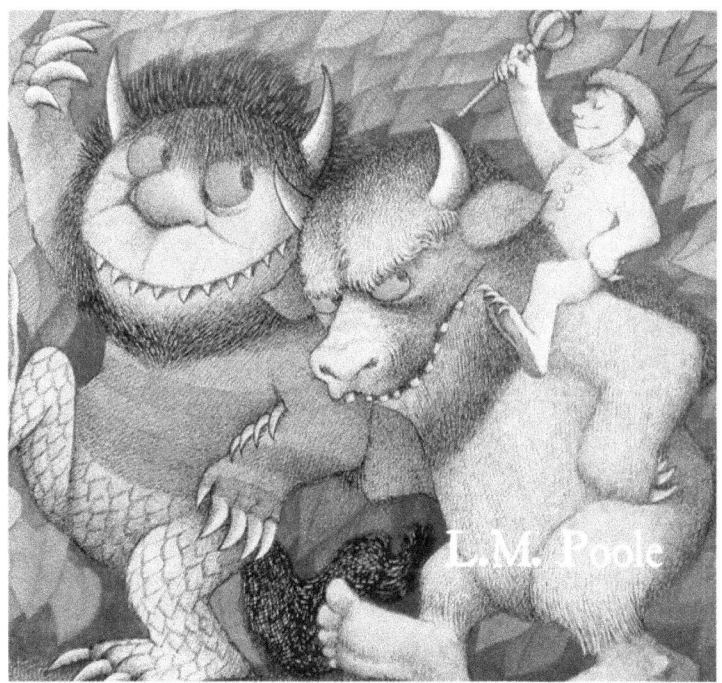

Maurice Sendak is the widely acclaimed American children's book author and illustrator. This critical study focuses on his famous trilogy, *Where the Wild Things Are*, *In the Night Kitchen* and *Outside Over There*, as well as the early works and Sendak's superb depictions of the Grimm Brothers' fairy tales in *The Juniper Tree*. L.M. Poole begins with a chapter on children's book illustration, in particular the treatment of fairy tales. Sendak's work is situated within the history of children's book illustration, and he is compared with many contemporary authors.

Fully illustrated. The book has been revised and updated for this edition.
ISBN 9781861714282 Pbk   ISBN 9781861713469 Hbk

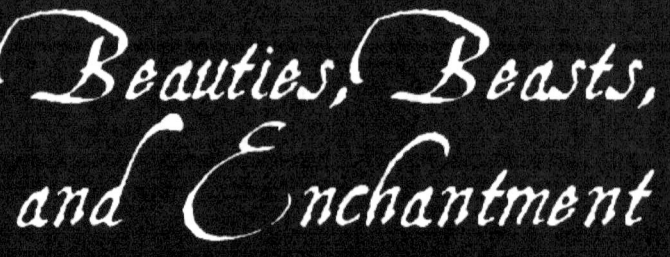

Beauties, Beasts, and Enchantment

CLASSIC FRENCH FAIRY TALES

Translated and with an Introduction
by Jack Zipes

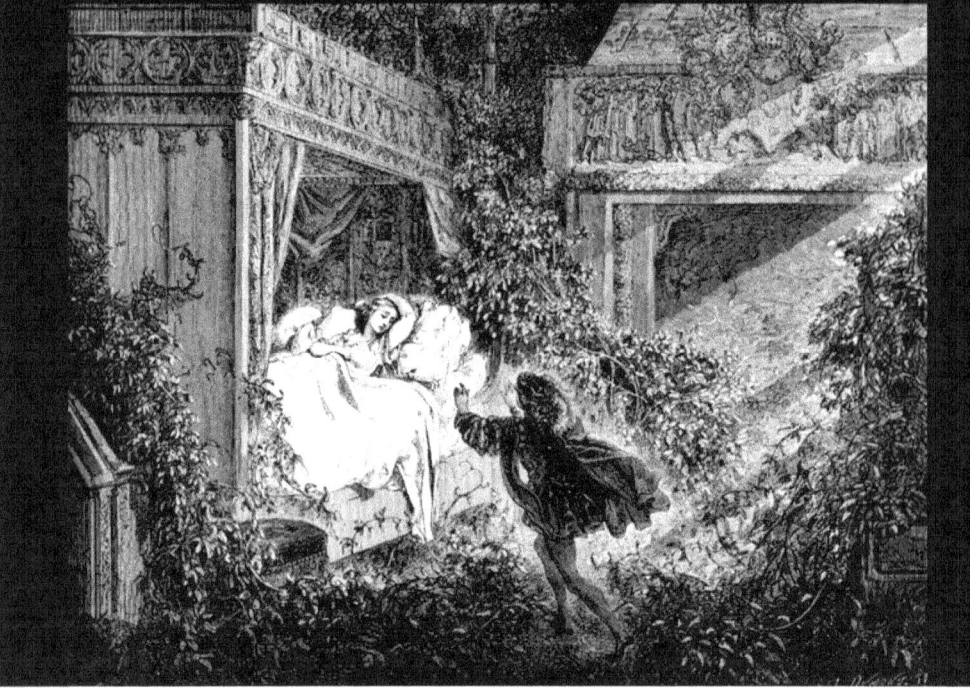

A collection of 36 classic French fairy tales translated by renowned writer Jack Zipes.
Cinderella, Beauty and the Beast, Sleeping Beauty and *Little Red Riding Hood* are among the
classic fairy tales in this amazing book.
Includes illustrations from fairy tale collections.
Jack Zipes has written and published widely on fairy tales.

'Terrific... a succulent array of 17th and 18th century 'salon' fairy tales'
- *The New York Times Book Review*

'These tales are adventurous, thrilling in a way fairy tales are meant to be... The translation
from the French is modern, happily free of archaic and hyperbolic language... a fine and
sophisticated collection' - *New York Tribune*

'Enjoyable to read... a unique collection of French regional folklore' - *Library Journal*

'Charming stories accompanied by attractive pen-and-ink drawings' - *Chattanooga Times*

Introduction and illustrations   612pp.   ISBN 9781861712510 Pbk   ISBN 9781861713193 Hbk

CRESCENT MOON PUBLISHING

web: www.crmoon.com e-mail: cresmopub@yahoo.co.uk

ARTS, PAINTING, SCULPTURE

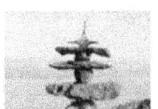
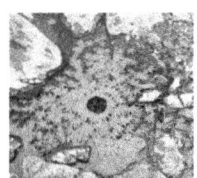

The Art of Andy Goldsworthy
Andy Goldsworthy: Touching Nature
Andy Goldsworthy in Close-Up
Andy Goldsworthy: Pocket Guide
Andy Goldsworthy In America
Land Art: A Complete Guide
The Art of Richard Long
Richard Long: Pocket Guide
Land Art In the UK
Land Art in Close-Up
Land Art In the U.S.A.
Land Art: Pocket Guide
Installation Art in Close-Up
Minimal Art and Artists In the 1960s and After
Colourfield Painting
Land Art DVD, TV documentary
Andy Goldsworthy DVD, TV documentary
The Erotic Object: Sexuality in Sculpture From Prehistory to the Present Day
Sex in Art: Pornography and Pleasure in Painting and Sculpture
Postwar Art
Sacred Gardens: The Garden in Myth, Religion and Art
Glorification: Religious Abstraction in Renaissance and 20th Century Art
Early Netherlandish Painting
Leonardo da Vinci
Piero della Francesca
Giovanni Bellini
Fra Angelico: Art and Religion in the Renaissance
Mark Rothko: The Art of Transcendence
Frank Stella: American Abstract Artist
Jasper Johns
Brice Marden
Alison Wilding: The Embrace of Sculpture
Vincent van Gogh: Visionary Landscapes
Eric Gill: Nuptials of God
Constantin Brancusi: Sculpting the Essence of Things
Max Beckmann
Caravaggio
Gustave Moreau
Egon Schiele: Sex and Death In Purple Stockings
Delizioso Fotografico Fervore: Works In Process 1
Sacro Cuore: Works In Process 2
The Light Eternal: J.M.W. Turner
The Madonna Glorified: Karen Arthurs

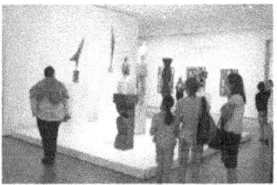
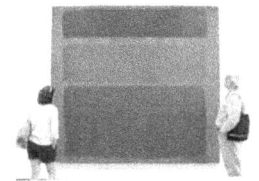
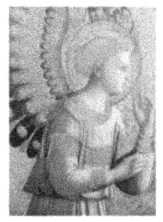
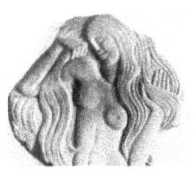
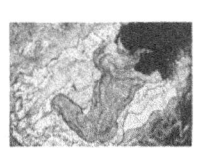
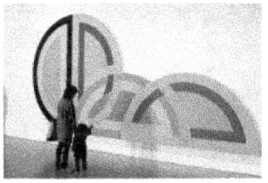
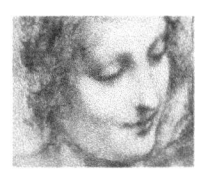
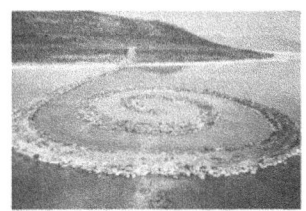

LITERATURE

J.R.R. Tolkien: The Books, The Films, The Whole Cultural Phenomenon
J.R.R. Tolkien: Pocket Guide
Tolkien's Heroic Quest
The *Earthsea* Books of Ursula Le Guin
Beauties, Beasts and Enchantment: Classic French Fairy Tales
German Popular Stories by the Brothers Grimm
Philip Pullman and *His Dark Materials*
Sexing Hardy: Thomas Hardy and Feminism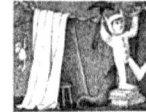
Thomas Hardy's *Tess of the d'Urbervilles*
Thomas Hardy's *Jude the Obscure*
Thomas Hardy: The Tragic Novels
Love and Tragedy: Thomas Hardy
The Poetry of Landscape in Hardy
Wessex Revisited: Thomas Hardy and John Cowper Powys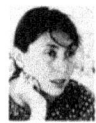
Wolfgang Iser: Essays and Interviews
Petrarch, Dante and the Troubadours
Maurice Sendak and the Art of Children's Book Illustration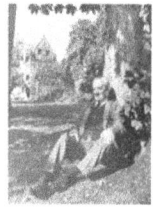
Andrea Dworkin
Cixous, Irigaray, Kristeva: The *Jouissance* of French Feminism
Julia Kristeva: Art, Love, Melancholy, Philosophy, Semiotics and Psychoanalysis
Hélène Cixous I Love You: The *Jouissance* of Writing
Luce Irigaray: Lips, Kissing, and the Politics of Sexual Difference
Peter Redgrove: Here Comes the Flood
Peter Redgrove: Sex-Magic-Poetry-Cornwall
Lawrence Durrell: Between Love and Death, East and West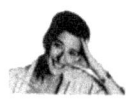
Love, Culture & Poetry: Lawrence Durrell
Cavafy: Anatomy of a Soul
German Romantic Poetry: Goethe, Novalis, Heine, Hölderlin
Feminism and Shakespeare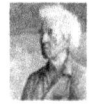
Shakespeare: Love, Poetry & Magic
The Passion of D.H. Lawrence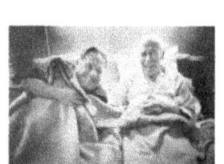
D.H. Lawrence: Symbolic Landscapes
D.H. Lawrence: Infinite Sensual Violence
Rimbaud: Arthur Rimbaud and the Magic of Poetry
The Ecstasies of John Cowper Powys
Sensualism and Mythology: The Wessex Novels of John Cowper Powys
Amorous Life: John Cowper Powys and the Manifestation of Affectivity (H.W. Fawkner)
Postmodern Powys: New Essays on John Cowper Powys (Joe Boulter)
Rethinking Powys: Critical Essays on John Cowper Powys
Paul Bowles & Bernardo Bertolucci
Rainer Maria Rilke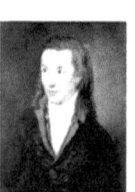
Joseph Conrad: *Heart of Darkness*
In the Dim Void: Samuel Beckett
Samuel Beckett Goes into the Silence
André Gide: Fiction and Fervour
Jackie Collins and the Blockbuster Novel
Blinded By Her Light: The Love-Poetry of Robert Graves
The Passion of Colours: Travels In Mediterranean Lands
Poetic Forms

POETRY

Ursula Le Guin: Walking In Cornwall
Peter Redgrove: Here Comes The Flood
Peter Redgrove: Sex-Magic-Poetry-Cornwall
Dante: Selections From the Vita Nuova
Petrarch, Dante and the Troubadours
William Shakespeare: Sonnets
William Shakespeare: Complete Poems
Blinded By Her Light: The Love-Poetry of Robert Graves
Emily Dickinson: Selected Poems
Emily Brontë: Poems
Thomas Hardy: Selected Poems
Percy Bysshe Shelley: Poems
John Keats: Selected Poems
Joh n Keats: Poems of 1820
D.H. Lawrence: Selected Poems
Edmund Spenser: Poems
Edmund Spenser: Amoretti
John Donne: Poems
Henry Vaughan: Poems
Sir Thomas Wyatt: Poems
Robert Herrick: Selected Poems
Rilke: Space, Essence and Angels in the Poetry of Rainer Maria Rilke
Rainer Maria Rilke: Selected Poems
Friedrich Hölderlin: Selected Poems
Arseny Tarkovsky: Selected Poems
Arthur Rimbaud: Selected Poems
Arthur Rimbaud: A Season in Hell
Arthur Rimbaud and the Magic of Poetry
Novalis: Hymns To the Night
German Romantic Poetry
Paul Verlaine: Selected Poems
Elizaethan Sonnet Cycles
D.J. Enright: By-Blows
Jeremy Reed: Brigitte's Blue Heart
Jeremy Reed: Claudia Schiffer's Red Shoes
Gorgeous Little Orpheus
Radiance: New Poems
Crescent Moon Book of Nature Poetry
Crescent Moon Book of Love Poetry
Crescent Moon Book of Mystical Poetry
Crescent Moon Book of Elizabethan Love Poetry
Crescent Moon Book of Metaphysical Poetry
Crescent Moon Book of Romantic Poetry
Pagan America: New American Poetry

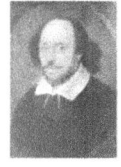
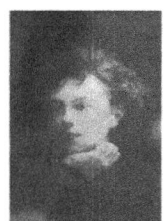
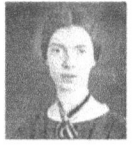
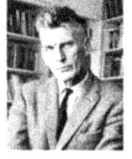

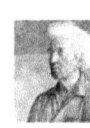
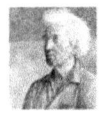
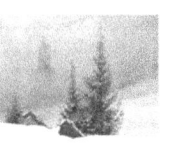
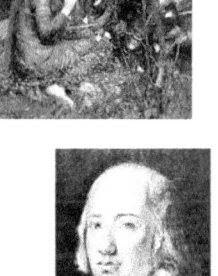
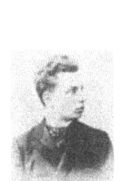
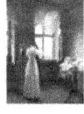
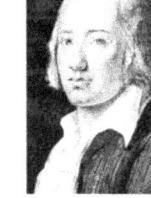

MEDIA, CINEMA, FEMINISM and CULTURAL STUDIES

J.R.R. Tolkien: The Books, The Films, The Whole Cultural Phenomenon
J.R.R. Tolkien: Pocket Guide
The *Lord of the Rings* Movies: Pocket Guide
The Cinema of Hayao Miyazaki
Hayao Miyazaki: *Princess Mononoke*: Pocket Movie Guide
Hayao Miyazaki: *Spirited Away*: Pocket Movie Guide
Tim Burton : Hallowe'en For Hollywood
Ken Russell

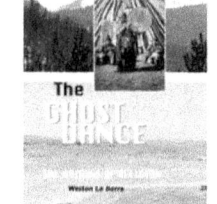

Ken Russell: *Tommy*: Pocket Movie Guide
The Ghost Dance: The Origins of Religion
The Peyote Cult
Cixous, Irigaray, Kristeva: The *Jouissance* of French Feminism
Julia Kristeva: Art, Love, Melancholy, Philosophy, Semiotics and Psychoanalysis
Luce Irigaray: Lips, Kissing, and the Politics of Sexual Difference
Hélene Cixous I Love You: The *Jouissance* of Writing
Andrea Dworkin

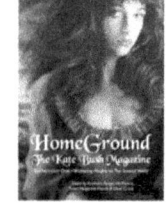

'Cosmo Woman': The World of Women's Magazines
Women in Pop Music
HomeGround: The Kate Bush Anthology
Discovering the Goddess (Geoffrey Ashe)
The Poetry of Cinema
The Sacred Cinema of Andrei Tarkovsky

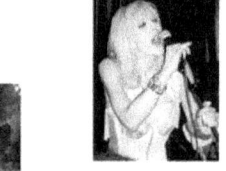

Andrei Tarkovsky: Pocket Guide
Andrei Tarkovsky: *Mirror*: Pocket Movie Guide
Andrei Tarkovsky: *The Sacrifice*: Pocket Movie Guide
Walerian Borowczyk: Cinema of Erotic Dreams
Jean-Luc Godard: The Passion of Cinema
Jean-Luc Godard: *Hail Mary*: Pocket Movie Guide

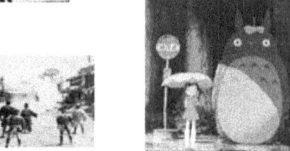

Jean-Luc Godard: *Contempt*: Pocket Movie Guide
Jean-Luc Godard: *Pierrot le Fou*: Pocket Movie Guide
John Hughes and Eighties Cinema
Ferris Bueller's Day Off: Pocket Movie Guide
Jean-Luc Godard: Pocket Guide
The Cinema of Richard Linklater

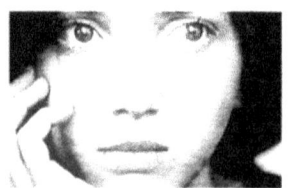

Liv Tyler: Star In Ascendance
Blade Runner and the Films of Philip K. Dick
Paul Bowles and Bernardo Bertolucci
Media Hell: Radio, TV and the Press
An Open Letter to the BBC
Detonation Britain: Nuclear War in the UK
Feminism and Shakespeare
Wild Zones: Pornography, Art and Feminism
Sex in Art: Pornography and Pleasure in Painting and Sculpture
Sexing Hardy: Thomas Hardy and Feminism

The Light Eternal is a model monograph, an exemplary job. The subject matter of the book is beautifully organised and dead on beam. (Lawrence Durrell)
It is amazing for me to see my work treated with such passion and respect. (Andrea Dworkin)

CRESCENT MOON PUBLISHING
P.O. Box 1312, Maidstone, Kent, ME14 5XU, Great Britain. www.crmoon.com

cresmopub@yahoo.co.uk   www.crescentmoon.org.uk

www.ingramcontent.com/pod-product-compliance
Lightning Source LLC
Chambersburg PA
CBHW051325220526
45468CB00004B/1503